THE OTHER SHORE

Picas Series 4

ANTONIO D'ALFONSO

The OTHER SHORE

Illustrated with Photographs by the Author

GUERNICA

Some of these poems have appeared in
Other Channels,
Dix poètes anglophones du Québec (Voix-Off),
*Lèvres Urbaines, Il Caffè (California), Vice Versa,
Quêtes: Textes d'auteurs italo-québécois,
Poetry Agenda 1984, Poetry Canada Review,
Canadian Literature* and *Apeuropa* (Rome).

Copyright © 1986, 1988 by Antonio D'Alfonso
First published in this Format in 1988.
Photocomposition by Atelier LHR
Legal Deposit — second quarter
Bibliothèque nationale du Québec
& National Library of Canada

Guernica Editions, P.O. Box 633,
Station N.D.G., Montréal (Québec),
Canada H4A 3R1

Guernica Editions gratefully acknowledge
financial support from Multiculturalism Canada,
The Canada Council and le ministère des Affaires culturelles

Canadian Cataloguing in Publication Data

D'Alfonso, Antonio, 1953-
The other shore

(Picas series; 4)
ISBN 0-920717-32-2

I. Title. II. Series.

PS8557.A456084 1988   C811'.54   C88-090253-1
PR9199.3.D34084 1988

Contents

Note	7
L'UOMO SOLO	
Pry the Filth Off Your Maps	13
To Drink the Act in Motion	15
Passion and its Inebriety	16
The Flakiness of Words	17
You Refuse to Write	18
There Will Never Be a Promised Land	19
Where Is the Meaning in All This?	21
Sunday in Room Six	22
Burning Our Fingers	25
Ghiaccio	26
BEYOND MY LIMITS	
The Men Upstairs	29
Lonely Women, Lonely Men	30
Dues	31
The Mouth Is Blind	32
Easter Sunday	33
The Machine	35
Violare	36
Vocabularies	38
An der Lühe, 6	40
Aut Hausen Strasse	42
Im Sachsenhausen	44
The People Across the Street	46
The Wooden Plank	48
Amarti così lontana	50
GUGLIONESI	
Babel	57
Where Do I Begin?	58
To Maintain Your Identity	59
The Loss of a Culture	60
The Family	61
Guglionesi	62
Sant'Adamo Came Here	64
Il vero divorzio è l'emigrazione	65
Who Are We?	67
Living Beside Santa Maria Maggiore	69

Nonna Lucia	71
Camaleonte	73
On Being a Wop	74
Per Antonio	76
The Look of a Child	78
My Mother's Advice	80
Simmetria	81
La tua fotografia	82
Italia Mea Amore	84

ROMAMOR

She	91
Italia-Express	92
An Eroticism of Words	93
Our Continent	94
For Our Children	96
Trees	97
Se son rose, fioriranno	98
Bindings	99
Will Passion Ever Forget Me?	100

TO CRITICIZE ONESELF

The Poverty of Money	105
On Writing	106
The Purity of Thinking	114
For Louis Dudek	115
New Economics	118
The Critic and the Poet	120
Apatride	122
To Criticize Oneself	123

SIX

Roma-Montréal	129
Roma	131
Barbara Engelmann in Arezzo	134
I Cannot Write as I Used To	136
Per Pier Giorgio Di Cicco	139
Ostia-Lido: Per Pier Paolo Pasolini	142

IL NUOVO BAROCCO

Il Nuovo Barocco	147

Note

Italiam non sponte sequor.
(I am pushed towards Italy and it is
beyond my control.)
Virgil
Aeneid, IV, 361

This book of broken verses, broken thoughts, about broken feelings. This, a notebook without a beginning, without an end, only a flowing towards being, a growing; contradictions and explanations. This, my *Made in Italy*, my *Portrait of an Italian*, my *Returning Home*, my *Italia-Express*; this, my *Do Not Throw Anything Out the Window*, my *The Lone Man*, my *There Is No Promised Land*. This notebook was written between March 1984 and June 1985, with the addition of fragments composed as early as 1979. This book would not have been possible without the presence of Claude Beausoleil, Philippe Haeck, Luigi Luzio and Patrick Straram.

Music I listened to while writing these texts: Enzo Avitabile: *Meglio Soul* and *Correre in fretta*; Franco Battiato: *L'era del cinghiale bianco*, *Patriots*, *La voce del padrone*, *L'Arca di Noè*, *Orizzonti perduti* and *Mondi lontanissimi*; Lucio Battisti's Collected Songs; Fabio Concato's songs; Lucio Dalla: *4 marzo e altre storie*, *Dalla*, *L'anno che verrà*, *1983* and *Viaggi organizzati*; Pino Daniele: *Musicante*; Alberto Fortis: *El niño*; Matia Bazar: *Tango* and *Aristocratica*; Gianna Nannini: *Puzzle*; Vasco Rossi: *Va bene, va bene così*; Luigi Tenco's Collected Songs; Antonello Venditti: *Circo Massimo* and *Cuore*.

L'UOMO SOLO

Pour Philippe Haeck

*L'uomo solo ascolta la voce antica
che i suoi padri, nei tempi, hanno udito, chiara
e raccolta, una voce che come il verde
degli stagni e dei colli incupisce a sera.*
Cesare Pavese
«La casa»

Pry the Filth Off Your Maps

The fear of being shot at. Leaders walk behind us. We talk with their voices, hypodermic needles in our arms. Their loudspeakers, anonymous. We hear but do not listen. We fill our pockets with pills because we are frightened. Do not step on us, we are not worms. Who keeps the hands of the dial apart? Who has stuffed our ears with newspapers?

Basta. Show reality as it is. Not through the eyes of a blind reporter. The running around, the stumbling over, the hang-over. The curiosity of knowing the further shore. The feasts across the borders, the kissing behind the backs of victims. The villagers' hands upturned to the sky in awe.

To stuff the veins of foreigners with mud is a source of violence, flattens the perspective in history. It takes dedication to discipline the confusion in our homes. If you talk to strangers, do not yawn. Listen to the humility of their temper. Dice your imagination. Pry the filth off your maps. Feel the relief.

6 May 1981

To Drink the Act in Motion

I do not easily fall asleep. Too much sleep only makes me sleepy. I need to stand on edge like a nervous trapeze artist or as someone looking down from the World Trade Centre. I need to feel dizzy, sense the uncertainty of feelings and ideas. "Strike me with your whip." But I am neither someone who wants to hit nor a victim. I want to be in between the executioner's whip and the victim's back, between the strength of the arm and the vulnerability of the waiting skin. I want to find myself standing on the wire of action, inside action. In the realism of motion. After action begins, before action comes to its conclusion. I want to be lost in the inebriety of the instant, in the giddiness of motion. I need to drink the act of motion, and fall asleep drunk.

9 June 1983

Passion and its Inebriety

Passion and its inebriety. The insecurity of signs. What limits do you impose on yourself when the moon is torn to pieces? It is not so much love has not rung you up yet that depresses you, as much as your unemployed body. The bags some fill with their riches are tougher than you thought. The instruments you play with become obsolete. The images of someone you used to be, the images of someone you will be. The noon-break alarm makes you salivate as if you had never seen food before.

The Flakiness of Words

The flakiness of words. What peels off or can be chipped. Words wear down. They lose their thickness and crumble, exhausted. After dogs and scientists take their bite into them, what is left for women? A great tendency to excessive reduction: to darken the gamut of possible meaning. Even the outrageous word has the right to be a metaphor. I like words that shock, words that purposely push you off balance. Hysterical words. Their power or lack of power is my freedom. I know a word can only be a metaphor. If it is not, why do we spend so much time building whatever it is we are trying to build?

You Refuse to Write

You can refuse to write but it is not as simple as some make it to be. Language is a voice that answers your questions, that questions your answers. It is a killing. Nothing easy. Look at a window whose curtains have been drawn, the fabric swaying in the wind, its folds as deep as a head lost in thought. Hear the nervous footsteps of someone fighting with words. A hand grabs the killer on the scene of the crime. That is when a day of work ends and when the night of words begins. Paper as dense as prayers, and as mute. Paper that you will bind or burn. All around walls of paper you cannot climb, with only one window to look out of. Language has put it there for you to stare at the world without words.

There Will Never Be a Promised Land

There will never be a promised land.
There will never be dreams sitting
beside you, holding your hand, in the subway car.

When the patient speaks you will
only hear the whispers of frustration,
the sighs of someone who does not care.

You will hear the screeching of brains
on the wet macadam. You will see
blood everywhere and you will eat it.

It will be now and here. When and where
people wear band-aids on their mouths,
jewelry on their necks like chains,

driving cars like tanks across our lands.
There is no leader who speaks
the same language as you.

You will learn the codes, the syntax
and vocabulary, but you will have
been used by them and not using them.

> The meat that you eat,
> the blood that you drink,
> are your own flesh and blood.

24 May 1983

Where Is the Meaning in All This?

Where is the meaning of all this? The refusal, poverty or wealth, to go beyond the outlines of craters? Seeing the flat sun tear like paper. Fibers the few workers that remain would like to cover. With their love, sperm, blood. Where is the meaning in the dialects we invent for ourselves to converse in? The language of the tribe cannot be purified, and if once it could have been no one cares to do so today. Poverty or wealth, this audacity of wanting to ornament our borders, national and personal? Strike, strike down those words we have modelled like straightjackets. Who can turn a signified to a signifer in our liquid sky?

Sunday in Room Six

1

This room, number six,
lonely as the only
hotel in this little town,

with a sink large enough
to wash the drunkenness
from your face.

A tiny desk with too many books
and not enough space for
this sheet to write on.

A bed beneath the only window,
where voices roll up
like a cat's tail at your leg.

English voices
of French girls
giggling at boys' advances.

An air-conditioner switched on
for noisy fresh-air, switched off
for stuffy silence.

2

The church bells toll noon,
time for Mass,
a mass none may skip.

The dog under my window sill
howls its complaint
to its immutable god.

Can one be the free wind
pushing its way
through wheat swaths?

The heart is ripped
like the sinus
by this skunk-smelling rain.

3

Te quiero cuando en el fondo
del vacio la noche llora.
Sí, te quiero con estas manos
rojas de perro herido.
Aún tú vienes con boca llena
de luna iluminada, sola,
sonriendo con la luz del sol.

4

*The moon is a patch in the sky.
The night closes in on you
and is a fist you want to open.*

It knocks at your door late one night
when you think you are alone.
It is a stare that goes right
to the pain hidden behind your glasses.
It speaks words you have heard before
but which are now fruit
you taste for the first time.
It brushes against you and strikes
your life like a match.
You crumple your fear, a note
you have become ashamed of.
You hope to keep it, a promise,
a ticket in your wallet.

*It is the moon, it is the night,
it slips away pretending
it does not recognize you.*

1980-1982

Burning Our Fingers

Morality as personal solution. A way of getting out of accidents. Morals are not morality. They are what nuclear warfare is to uranium. What you decide is good for you is one outcome of numberless possibilities. An outcome is always ephemeral. You have to find your way of connecting yourself to me so that the light goes on. Sunlamps can be interesting but I need a brightness which only the instant sparks off. Once I did not care if I was struck by thunder, now I keep away from its blast. We are children who have learned that fire burns our fingers.

5 October 1983

Ghiaccio

I am ice. I thaw with time. With heat. And become what I originally was. Why does the ocean fascinate me so much? I sit before the Saint-Laurent and the Biferno. Before the Tevere and the Arno. Before the German Main and the Po. I taste the Atlantic and the Pacific. I taste the Tyrrhenian and the Adriatic. I drink polluted water and am cleansed by it. Water, never still, always changing, cannot be imprisoned by matter or metaphor. Water for mother, freedom, nomadism, the unconscious. Where I begin. Where I will find myself in the end — if there is an end. How deep is the ocean? How deep the ocean in me? How deep is the ocean I swim in?

6 June 1984

BEYOND MY LIMITS

The Men Upstairs

Pour Richard Lamer

The men upstairs are discussing,
they are fighting about what can
and cannot be done. The men upstairs
are not normal. We say they have
emotional and physical problems.
The men are not normal
because we have made them that way.

This is a house for epileptics.
We call them outsiders, men
without homes. They know what
kind of hearth they can run to.
The men upstairs go in circles.
They like and use other men,
they like and use what is available.

The men are upstairs because
they find nothing downstairs except
the normal men, except an unkempt office.
There is a typewriter, there is a man.
The words he strikes on the keyboard
are the words the men upstairs
would like to use but can't.

14 February 1982

Lonely Women, Lonely Men

They stay clumped together, in the middle of kitchens, talking quietly of work and politics. "It is not the managing of a household of three by myself that kills me." They do not suffer from solitude: they have friends — folded paper with phone numbers in wallets — who run to lift them from the floor, when they have swallowed too many pills. They speak about themselves as employers scolding their employees. "I understand you, I have slept with the devil as well." They sit quietly in living rooms, drinking mint tea or Campari soda, whispering how it is easier to live with someone of your own sex. Silence falls, a wine glass on the marble floor. They find this stranger sleeping in the hallway, pants or skirt pulled to the knees. It is midnight, a lonely woman phones a lonely man, an order of five-minute sex.

February 1985

Dues

This man dresses to be bought. "You're running, you're running." He has been late from the start. A bag of dead cells unable to fulfil their duty. They pay the price he is worth. So much for this, so much for that. Who tackles him left and right? His hair thinning, a close-up calling for a poet's inspiration. How much are you asking for him? His dues: a woman's self-smothered orgasm? A man's torn sphincter?

18 June 1985

The Mouth Is Blind

Word-blindness. Dyslexia. He confuses born and porn, bed and dead. She inverts letters and sounds, forgetting there are foundations He is not allowed to prick or break. Sounds pronounced as letters not there. Words for things never mentioned. She is blind, or should I say, His mouth is blind. She cannot differentiate one letter from another. When He goes in a tank She really means bank. If She meets you He shakes your hand and says stank, instead of thanks.

27 November 1983

Easter Sunday

From one room to another. Falling. "What are you running after?" Comfort, simple comfort. Do not look at the mess. Be ready to lift what you refused to carry up till now. Red pencils marking the worst of your efforts. Which room shall you paint first? "No, I will not give in. You are pushing me out of my comfort."

All this crying — why? Breaking rules, respecting laws. The outlaw reinforces the laws he wants torn to pieces. Patience. What if the world is a song after all? A way to happiness. A vision. Or grace. Odour of sweating bodies. Flesh wrung like clothes. Exertion. The pain of controlling what was believed uncontrollable, or worse, natural. Voices loud in their suppressed anger. The wrenching of what is supposed to be inborn. Plans thrown on the floor like dishes.

Faces knock against the rim of glasses. Voices, words, eyes that refuse to meet. Her eyes green, the colour of the wall behind her. Hair burning. Red hues in the Persian carpet, red lipstick on her half-opened lips, red nail-polish on her fingers that never touched his black earth. Sephardic blue. She sits. Stands. Sits. Her hand grazes the thin line separating the noise and melody. The feeding of one desire at a time. The world and guts. Easter Sunday, the weather as metaphor. Will the crying become music? *How long it has taken me to come to you.* *

---

* An allusion to Robert Bresson (*Pickpocket*), Paul Schrader (*American Gigolo*) and Jean-Luc Godard (*Je vous salue, Marie*).

The Machine

Are they going to live on Mars? Or take off to some further star? This is no illusion. Somebody wears an astronaut's outfit and waits for the blast-off. His hands are on a computer keyboard, and out comes music. He loves this machine more than his wife. This is good. Give him the money he needs and he will find a better world. Machine is not a synonym for war. It has its own soul and feels oppressed when mistreated. What rules has the poet broken now? He goes down on his machine and makes it come. This too is love. The centre of gravity is not up in the clouds. Give the machine land and it will grow tomatoes and zucchini, a world resembling very much our own. The corners of the square have been rounded off to a circumference. No law is natural, no nature is law.

8 June 1983

Violare

Violence does not rhyme with dance but with defence. Some walk into the world on their tiptoes, exit with a scream. Others enter screaming and walk out on their tiptoes. The hypothesis is unbending. You see red and charge like a bull. Only the eyes of your enemies glare at you, dizzy buttons. "You can talk about it until you turn blue and green, but if you do not experience it you know nothing of violence." The body speaks. Its rhetorics have nothing to do with the eloquence of speech or the refinery of perfumes and clothes. No wonder we associate sports, sex and violence. One source: to rape a woman or to strike the player on the opposite team. You are raping me. *Violare*, in Latin. Who plays that viola d'amore? Words never make any sense. You have to turn them upside down and study them under a microscope. You have to love and not rape the vocabulary of humanity. *Tendebantque manus ripae ulterioris amore* (scrive Virgilio). Crossroads. To stand at crossroads, four friends inviting you, none less attractive than the other. Violence. The intensity the same at the cardinal points. The spell of waiting lasting beyond whatever you imagined lasting to be. Warm as a bed in the morning. What limits are there to going further away? An impatient drive slices you with the certainty of a blade. The four roads join hands to form a circle.

14 May 1981 / 15 September 1983

Vocabularies

1

G*oduria*: rapture or *jouissance*. To enjoy intensely. To accept orgasm. To feel like a god. *God*ere. God*ere*. To come. Before God. Rapture with existence. Rapture with God. With people, with words. *Lei gode*. Why is there no equivalent in English? She comes. It is time for poets to invent such a word.

2

T*erremoto*. Earthquakes in Italy. Chandeliers swinging not as in a dance but like heads severed by machine-gun bullets coming from tanks or stolen buses. To lose one's balance, the poet realizing how precarious is his art. Rumble one can actually see, thunder flashes inside the body. Earthquakes turn man into a bird. As solid as earth. As empty. Gravity as remote to him as dinosaurs. Floating in midair. What economy can bring him safely to solid ground? We have tried all the scientific words to avoid this disaster. Sold cocaine, young girls, young boys. We have speculated in real estate, forged passports. What bank can protect you from this anonymous phone call? It is neither man nor woman breathing heavily on the other end of the line, getting aroused by our fear or complaints. Someone has put a time bomb in our Mercedes. "O God save America and send us money to build the fortresses of our luxuries."

Guglionesi, 10 giugno 1984
Ostia-Lido, 22 ottobre 1984

An der Lühe, 6

A doll's house. A large yard. Its heart, you walk in, to your right, a maid's room. My room. I do not know a word of German, I want to hide my head like a bird hides its head under its wings. Rain. No tears. Only a fever, my way to lock the world out of me. Frau Schröde brings me hot tea. "Are you sure you do not want a pill? My husband was saved by a miracle. Who can say what is right or wrong nowadays? Had we a child it would have created a lot of trouble since I am Protestant and my husband Catholic. I never take tea before bedtime. But what is bedtime for a childless couple? We lived so long never stopping to think that perhaps we did too much thinking. To have children you must not think about them.

They have to come naturally.'' A doll's house, a large yard. As you walk in, a room to your right. A maid's room, a guest room, it could have been a child's room. The Schröde rent it out to foreigners. A proxy for 40 Deutschmarks. What are 40 Deutschmarks?

Frankfurt, 1 October 1984

Aut Hausen Strasse

Rush-hour. Breaking away from working hours. Like people walking to Sunday morning Mass. "Take your time to buy fish and fruit for tonight's supper." *Auf Wiedersehen*.

Traffic of quiet bicycles cutting through the October drizzle. "The sky darker than yesterday." On the radio, Robert Fripp and Brian Eno: *Swastika Girls*. Rush-hour of opened mouths whose screams we do not hear. Forgive.

Symbols of welfare or torture. Screams muffled by slow-motion bicycles. Add a few notes of bass right here. A brass section, followed by percussions. The camera does a slow travelling over the rush-hour of corpses.

An invisible narrator explains 1968 and how it felt to be a victim of flower-power propaganda, when American society underwent real radical changes. A pause. No regret for the death of the flower generation. "Pass the Bible. Lend me your syringe."

Symbols of democracy or totalitarianism. "How is it to live in the most democratic country on the planet?" The narrator screams. A tilt on to the macadam. Fade out on opened mouths. In pain. Old World, New World. Lunch break. Rush-hour of ideas, rush-hour of memories. "To change, to change, but we do not know what into."

9 October 1984

Im Sachsenhausen

> *La mia lingua/mi isolava/
> l'ho abbandonata/con la tua/
> imputridiscono/in me/i sensi.*
> Gino Chiellino

The language of one country in another country. Listen to the music coming in from the other room. Workers speak about the land in which they planted seeds of children and wives. Who knows what *father* and *mother* mean to them?

Not a question of nativeland. Our nativeland, a plane bringing us from point A to point B. Place, country: what do these mean to you, my love? Foreigner in a foreign land...

What do we desire from the soil of our bodies? Country without borders, country of our love. The language

we speak is the language of our bodies,
divided, united, poetry, poetry, why do
you make love like this? Always telling
me what I am not. Why do you come to
me this way? Unexpectedly.

The People Across the Street

A Lori e Pierre

People seen from my kitchen window. In the building right in front of ours. A man, his daughter fixing the water heater. Screwing it in and out all morning long. On the floor below, an elderly man filing a metal rod, every so often stopping to look at the people walking below his balcony. On the ground level, a mechanic smokes a cigarette, talking with a client, pointing towards the Tyrrhenian Sea. An old couple walks on Lungomare called Via del Duca degli Abruzzi — how can I escape from myself in Italy? Everywhere an image of myself... The woman on the fourth floor no longer in a red jumpsuit, now posing for me, for the man who is not her father. The elderly man on the floor below removes his glasses, goes inside his house. I am writing in a blue notebook, in blue ink, on a blue table. The mechanic fixes the blue sea. The woman stares at me, I turn my eyes away, hoping to catch a glimpse of myself coming around the corner.

Ostia, 19 October 1984

The Wooden Plank

A wooden plank found in the basement now burning in the fireplace. The fire slow at first, its fingers making their way through the cracks in little time. Fire, a hungry animal and not an evil man cracking his knuckles. Stare at the fire in the dark and see how it reaches for the sky. Compare fire to the screaming man cursing the gods. I am waiting for my love to get off the plane, I am waiting for my heart to walk back into the body it abandoned like an old barn.

Our love, a log you have to move in the fire. A little pushing and pulling to get the old gear in place. The wooden plank whispers, I do not know if in joy or pain. I do not know if love at thirty is something to jump and jive about. Whisper it to yourself, to your friends.

To appreciate fire you have to sleep beside it, listen to it purr like a kitten, its tiny paws caressing your face. The wind is warmer, the night sun boring holes in the carpet. I have left my English grammar book on my desk. I have put my dictionary back on the shelf. I am waiting for my love to come and push aside my fountain-pen, for what my love gives me no ink or paper can replace. I am waiting for love to consume me and turn me into something useful.

December 1984

Amarti così lontana

Drink a bottle of chilled white Frascati wine. Cold juice sinking into the pores of waiting. Inside the walls of an organism larger than the galaxy you float in. And yet be aware that all of this is nothing but a silly emotion. For all this nothing, this enactment of understanding, this misunderstanding procures you no pleasure, at least not the warm pleasure you experience when you sleep beside the body of love. Go to bed and pry open your pillow for the remains of love's odours. Mutter and spit because no utterance shall ever lift your body of love to its orgasm alone. The breathing. Only one breath, and not a second nor a third. Nothing but hot air talking inside the bar, the room where another body of love comes to open its desire to you. What oil mixes with water? What marriage of elements possible in this trigonometry of absence? Possibilities multiplied by your everyday incapacity to free yourself from lonely words, lonely explanations, intellectualizations about what cannot be contained by the heart. No beauty of creation. No creation can recreate love and its magical body. Not even creativity with wings. The breaking of the unbreakable. Becoming and becoming whatever it is you need to be. To stop because you have to. To continue believing that love possesses a body just for you. A breathing which becomes someone else. To say, This might very well work, though the translation be impure. This works because it can be itself, in itself. This continuing, this waking up. This putting yourself in parenthesis, under a cold shower, to cool down the fiery coals in your skull. No drink, no work, no passion to make you forget what you are, what you are living for, what reality belongs to you. Belonging to and not to belong to anything, anyone. Say Lord, yes Lord. To pray for the sake of praying, for the sake of writing a poem that will vanish the moment it is written. The air going up to heaven. To believe in life, and not imitate the life of your neighbour. If you have to imitate, let it be the body of love. The angel who guards this body. Say Lord, it is hard to live outside the body of love, abiding in the rules of selfishness and who-cares-about-tomorrow. To say so many words, to say nothing, to remain a soul looking for its body, out there, like a corpse which has received no funeral rite. Drink nothing. For nothing right can be drunk. This act of moving the mouth, only an enactment of the body of love you cannot have nor be. The presence, the presence... everywhere in your blood.

Montréal, 25 November 1984
Roma, 10 April 1985

GUGLIONESI

For Robert and Jason Carlo Trudeau

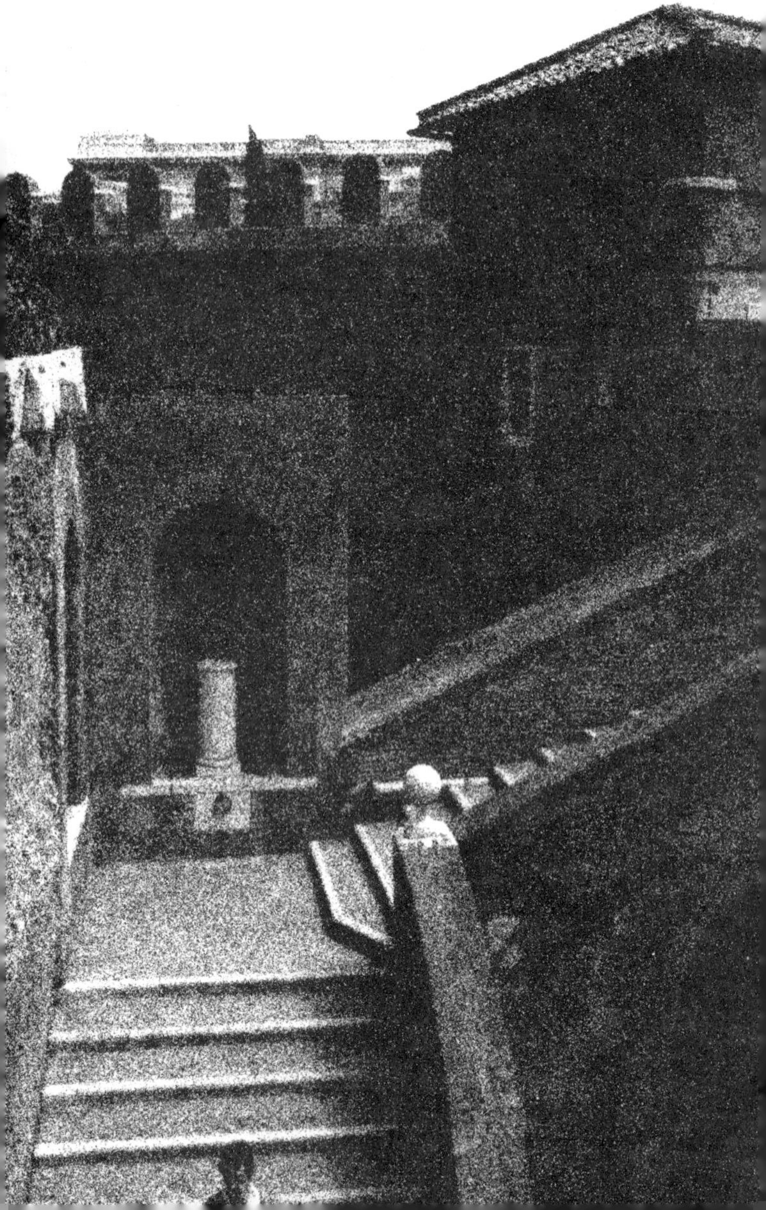

Se qualcuno mai ritorni nella terra dei padri troverà scritto tra le pietre e la gramigna, il grido dei morti e il pianto dei vivi, lontani.
                Francesco Jovine
                L'impero in provincia

C'è una ragione perché sono tornato in questo paese... Qui non ci sono nato, è quasi certo; dove son nato non lo so; non c'è da queste parti una casa né un pezzo di terra né delle ossa ch'io possa dire "Ecco cos'ero prima di nascere"... Chi può dire di che carne sono fatto? Ho girato abbastanza il mondo da sapere che tutte le carni sono buone e si equivalgono, ma è per questo che uno si stanca e cerca di mettere radici, di farsi terra e paese, perché la sua carne valga e duri qualcosa di più che un comune giro di stagione... Un paese ci vuole, non fosse che

per il gusto di andarsene via. Un paese vuol dire non essere soli, sapere che nella gente, nelle piante, nella terra c'è qualcosa di tuo, che anche quando non ci sei resta ad aspettarti.
                    Cesare Pavese
                    La luna e i falò

Je vais là où j'ai toujours su que j'irais. Ce qui me donne tout le temps nécessaire pour m'interroger sur le là *d'où je viens.*
                    André Beaudet
                    Littérature l'imposture

Babel

Nativo di Montréal
élevé comme Québécois
forced to learn the tongue of power
viví en México como alternativa
figlio del sole e della campagna
par les francs-parleurs aimé
finding thousands like me suffering
me casé y divorcié en tierra fria
nipote di Guglionesi
parlant politique malgré moi
steeled in the school of Old Aquinas
queriendo luchar con mis amigos latinos
Dio where shall I be demain
(trop vif) qué puedo saber yo
spero che la terra be mine

Where Do I Begin?

Where do I begin? Can I write *I* and not be criticized for being an egotist? Where does one begin? In which language to write? Which world to slip in? Who are you trying to get at? Who is your public? A nineteen-year-old girl? A forty-year-old man? The wind caressing your face? Is this the beginning I was looking for? Propoganda the goal of all art: which side are the left and right on? Where do I begin? In this landscape beneath the mighty Maiella? Is one moment to remember worth so much effort and concentration? The food, the dialect, the peoples? Where do I begin? Where do you come in?

Guglionesi, 4 giugno 1984

To Maintain Your Identity

"Do not kill me. Come back." The earth and water scream. The tuff and marble scream. The lizard changing from beachsand brown to vegetation-green. The snakes and palm-trees. The women and men out there in the autumn cold tilling the soil for fennel. And you are sitting on a bench writing about what prevents your people from liberating themselves. Immigrant peddlars sell you wares they stole from you during the night. Are you to believe rumours? Old witches' tales. You do not give in. You eat your soup-dipped bread and speak, between mouthfuls, to your cousin who has speech trouble. Your dialect: mixture of Frentani, Latin, French, Slav, German, Turkish, Arab. How easy is it for you to maintain your identity?

6 giugno 1984

The Loss of a Culture

Not the trip to a land where words are pronounced as you were taught to pronounce them. Not the adage your grandmother serves you at dinner. The language you speak as a child, flushed down the toilet bowl. Your mother-tongue sounds as foreign to you as any language you do not understand. Forgotten as the life-style you once had. Latin engraved on darkened school desks. What do you tell yourself when you find yourself alone at night? The uneaten bread becomes stale. The avoided meeting of a one-night stand, dreadful. Squashed tomatoe on the floor sinks into the tiles of your perfection. You forget the past but the past will not forget you. You sit on broken chairs and get cramps when you are about to say something intelligent. If you collapse and smash your head on the floor, it will not be from lack of proper diet, it will be your ancestors who will shoot you from behind.

1981

The Family

Images one does not want to see. Images of sterility, images of life. Miraculous progenity. Unrolling, a home-movie, a scroll. Every father a daughter, every mother a son. A family rejuvenating itself without hardening into a fossil. Bones prove that death does not sign with an X: the only son with only a son and no son. "I want to be modern. Drink down those images and forget them." Images one refuses to look at, images one has been taught are vulgar, stilted, trite. O miraculous progenity. O imaginative life. Who gives you power to put marble on quicksand, build cities on water? What stubbornness of creation. You give birth, enhance the chances of change. Inventor of possibilities.

Guglionesi

Do not worry if you do not know where Guglionesi is. Or Campobasso. Or Molise. Few Italians know. "Is it part of Italy? Or America?" This fortified medieval mountain town is found on the calf of the Boot. A river runs below it: the Biferno, which flows into the Adriatic. Before 1964 Molise was called Abruzzi. For many reasons, financial and political, my people thought it best to become independent. I will not boast about my culture. I want to enumerate energy sources: mental, physical, metaphysical energies that participate in the making of a person, of a country. "What are you talking about?" Sometimes it is better not to get involved in politics. I am thinking of Ovidio, Dante Gabriel Rossetti, Cristina Rossetti, Gabriele D'Annunzio, Francesco Jovine, Ignazio Silone, Giose Rimanelli, Filippo Salvatore, Marco Micone, Marco Fraticelli, Maria Di Michele, Maria Melfi, I am talking about these writers who today, in

Roma, Via Giorgio Scalia 12, at ten past ten, come to sit beside me, at my table, behind an open window. 20° Celsius. And they call this winter. No, this is the season of words, names, history.

Sant'Adamo Came Here

Sant'Adamo came here in the thirteenth century with the goal of conquering these cliffs Turks and Germans once possessed. There is too much to name to use adjectives. Where are the Frentani? The Nazi used Guglionesi as a look-out, so did the Scots and Americans. What language made it possible for these people to communicate? What language makes it possible for me to come to you? We do not speak the same grammar, though the words sound familiar. There are more of my people in Montréal than there are in Guglionesi. It hurts me. Little remains, and the little which does remain will soon disappear if we do not come back. Come back? There is no return, only a coming to, a coming towards. No linearity in experience or identity, only an awareness. The more I look ahead, the more I look inside. This is my geography.

Il vero divorzio è l'emigrazione

There are seven Catholic churches and one Evangelist church in Guglionesi. There once were as many as thirty-three. *Santa Maria Maggiore, San Nicola di Bari, Sant'Antonio, San Felice, La Chiesa dei Cappuccini, La Chiesa del Rosario, La Chiesa di Santa Rita, La Chiesa dei Moricelli*. Each one serves over 500 Christians. There are about 6000 inhabitants in this small town at 375 meters above sea level. I call this respect for differences. There are as many political parties. Every citizen has the right to seek his and her own Utopia. A new path to beat, a new way of life. There are about half a dozen addicts and as many alcoholics. The first steal car radios and siphon gas to pay their fix; the second work on land or in factories to pay for their daily drink. Yesterday we found a forty-year old junkie in his house hanging by the neck; he used his daughter's skipping rope. Once upon a time emigration seemed a valid excuse to run away from here. Today emigration makes us want to puke. Emigration has split more families apart than the Berlin wall. But no one speaks of this; it is not in style, and the metaphor is not refined enough. Emigration is my people's concentration camp. On the wall of one of our churches our teenagers painted this graffito in red: *Il vero divorzio è l'emigrazione*.

6 June 1984

Who Are We?

City administrators do what they can to provide work for our young. City administrators even create promotional campaigns calling back the people who left the region. City administrators do their best. If things do not change, our town will disappear in less than a hundred years. We the old, we the young, we the farmers, we the students, we the workers, we the unemployed, we the women, we the men: who are we? Why do we limit our use of Italian to the first few minutes of flirting and then go back to speaking our dialect? "Emigration, our opium, our religion. Emigration, the only political party to vote for. Emigration, money and search for wealth. Emigration, a new form of education. Emigration, our sexuality." Some countries are bloated frogs pretendings to be bulls. When we look at ourselves, we do not see pink and yellow satin ribbons in the sky. We do not see gondolas on red-coloured waters in our eyes. We see oil-stained faces and bags of tired skin under dog-wet eyes. We see our pants discoloured by polluted water, earth under our broken fingernails. If we smell it is not because we do not wash. Our body as clean as the earth we work, the water we row our boats on. It is our cousins abroad who smell of soap and expensive deodorants. How do you destroy the smell of life? When we sit in front of our television set at night, it is not because we have nothing to say to one another: we have so much to say that sometimes it is better not to speak. We choose to remain silent and smile at the lies people tell about us.

June 6, 1984

Living Beside Santa Maria Maggiore

Babbo, what does it feel like living with your father, mother and brother on Vico Carlo Diego Cini 6, before you become aware of what it takes to get your penis hard? You come here a thousand times to stare at the circledance of singing sparrows and listen to Santa Maria Maggiore strike six o'clock. School: what do your remember of that Mussolini building? A third-storey balustrade from which your brother Andrea is pushed. An alley separates your house and Santa Maria Maggiore, too small for a man to pass in, large enough for a child. How often do you piss here? Take refuge here when your mother spanks you? When German or American soldiers knock at your door looking for women? Curses and screams. You run out telling the world how they have turned the earth inside out. You lower your head in your mother's bosom to block out the roar of planes dropping their indifference on a land you bought with handkerchiefs of sweat. Not a beginning, not a loss, a period when you can no longer claim what is and is not yours. You become the tenant of your life. Even the girls and beaches you invite those girls to darken under the bombcasted sky. But there is Verdi, or someone who looks like him, conducting *Il Trovatore* in front of Santa Maria Maggiore. You stand beside your father, tall on your feet listening for hours, but you need water to wash out the fire in your veins. You search everywhere and find it nowhere. Until you embark on the Greek *Vulcan* with the promises of a land of water. And a necessary land of water you find. Yet what you have in your body no water can cool. The fire in your eyes lights everything, welding history and power back together again.

Nonna Lucia

Nonna Lucia lies in bed all day. Gets up only for the pure milk chocolate on the kitchen counter. Stares out the window, her green eyes covered by cataracts, catching a fleeting angel. So she tells us. "*I tolto u caffè?*"

Nonna Lucia always knows the time of day. The streets her children in America live on. Regains her calm when told she is the split image of my mother. Tonino laughs: "Is it true in Vasto where you were born, Nonna, a woman needs seven men before she is satisfied?"

Nonna Lucia's arms darkened by slow moving blood. Her face deathburnt against white hair pulled back in a chignon. She hears church bells. Sits up painfully. "Once I could carry more bushels of grapes than our mule."

Nonna Lucia's chapped lips reveal teeth broken by hot peppers. Crosses one leg over the other. Her thin fragile hand in mine. "God has forgotten me down here. Why is He not coming to take this tiny body away?"

Guglionesi, 6 June 1984

Camaleonte

Not to burn after living my existence, not a lone bird consuming itself in fire, to rise anew from ashes to start another existence, not a lover burning away in the fire of love. I refuse to die. Or become another. I engage myself to be the one I am. This, my struggle, my right to be. A continuation. The *here*, the *there*. One country for emotion, one country for finance. This, my dual nationality, my private enterprise. If economy brings us from here to there, our duty then to analyze this change in economical terms. *Termoli*: the building of a parking lot brought to a halt. An archeologist discovers a Roman tomb. How much of Italy lies buried under our soil? I do not want to be covered by earth before my time. If you have to compare me to an animal, let it be the living and sly chameleon, not the non-existent phoenix.

6 giugno 1984

On Being a Wop

Per Patrizia Di Pardo

Who can say what national pride means? The feel for people living here, though they need not necessarily care? Not to come back to this place. What is my excuse if not the fear of what this country would do to me? Born abroad, this is how the world wants it. But national pride? This place, this city, this territory: almost twenty-seven centuries old. O Italia, nation beyond nation, where will we take you now? You are not nervous when you walk among your citizens in Rome, Montreal or Frankfurt. You drink a few beers and are beyond the grasp of people who wish to talk to you. *Foro Romano*. You, tired for having demonstrated on Via Nazionale. Protesting against the Mafia and the Heroin Plague. You want this march to be more than just a testimony, you want to express your people's desire to change. People without boundaries, people with homes in every country. The meaning of being Italian? The meaning of being European? American? To reconcile yourself to the world you belong to. What reconciliation is possible in what makes up the contradictions of being? To be one thing, to be another: what choice have you today? (Cold Frascati wine against your teeth...) What does struggle stand for, if not the people who gave you birth? Peasants without lands who have voices not for singing but rumours blowing in the wind. The cultures of being what being can never again be. Here or there: cultureless identity. The Italian culture: what does it mean to be Italian today if you live outside Italy? "If you don't live in Italy, you're not Italian." What does such a phrase mean? What does it stand for? To be anywhere just as long as you live your culture. To keep your batteries in full charge in order to become what you essentially are.

Roma, 30 ottobre 1984

Per Antonio

Tony, as you want to be called, last seed of what is and will ever be, let no one belittle you. Do not believe you will become richer by leaving poverty behind. Poverty follows you wherever you go.

In the middle of the night, I hear you grunt and scratch yourself, the nerves inside your skin about to burst into a dream. Last of the last, first of the new, wake up to yourself, imaginary soils bear no fruit. That downpour shall eventually come. Send me your criticism if I mispronounce my name. Teach me the history I know nothing of. Do not expect to fly on dreams. Breathe your own body, drink the pleasure of the woman you love. Let her remind you where you belong. Words rot in my mouth, no text possible on the beauty of the coming to in this world. Not in Vietnam, not in

Nicaragua, not in the hamburger stand as clean as a new valium container. Not in my dress you cannot distinguish from my work-clothes. Not in a flavourless stew — O melting pot of frigidity. Between marriage and divorce, between marriage and solitude, the land of mixed extremes. The limbo of happy people holding on to one another without the need to kill. Between the yes and no, between the possible and the indecision, the old house of whispers. *L'amour eunuque n'est pas pour nous.*

"How hard is my originality? Does it turn you on?" O scribbler of unpublishable letters. O writer of weisswine. O living poem which does not rhyme with the endings of modern aseptic pleasures. I am no book of poems. I am scared. O organization, tell me what have you in store for me? I want to dance, I want you to enjoy yourself in the fabric of wishing.

Guglionesi, 8 June 1984

The Look of a Child

For Filippo Salvatore

The look of a child,
bright more with maturity
and vision than fun,
searches like hands
in the pockets of Father's trousers
with the same fervour
as when deciphering, later,
the contents of a verse
which has — even when
not fully understood —
the taste of sugared bread in a bowl
of warm milk in the morning.

A scrapbook opens up
to the world of intimate revelations.
That soccer ball is the universe
he tries to control but which
is kicked out of reach.
A torn jacket worn everyday
to school and play is mended
to the completeness of a fruit,
the suit of love, the scarf and tie,
clothes for dignity.

The kiss and prayer marry at last
and a song lifts the look of growth
to the heart of rapture
where are born verse,
children and conscious innocence.

27 January 1981

My Mother's Advice

Nothing comes from single attempts, nothing fruitful from improvisation. The free gesture is only a glimpse of genius. One must be part of this and one must be far from this. Free oneself from oppressive fashions. The depth of conversation can be felt after years of talk around the same table, like students working out a mathematical equation. Pleasure, the aim of discipline. Even this must never remain the same: every end leads to unknown directions. A kiss is not savoured fully on the first night, nor the kiss a pen gives to the whiteness of paper. It takes many kisses to arrive at this moment of ecstasy, temporary ecstacy. Easiness is no promise of success. The wine on my lips has the flavour of sweat.

5 July 1981

Simmetria

Some days sentences come to me ready-made. I go for a walk and sit beside old men with canes in their trembling hands under wrinkled chins, as if to balance never-aging thoughts. *Large delle mura*. Below us, a valley of abstraction beneath snowtipped mountains. The symmetry of work. Nothing fictitious about man-power. Rolling vines around sticks in dry earth, the working into a garden, lettuce in cracked, calloused hands, the dreamy odour of cut grain, the poem. I put my pen down and walk inside my own symmetry. To shape my landscape against the rolling patterns in the sky. To slide my fingers in the sleeping earth and awaken with my saliva the world's sex.

Guglionesi, 6 giugno 1984

La tua fotografia

Per A.

Your head slightly bent to the right. Your right side darker than the left (at least that is how you appear on this photograph). You wear a black dress, *braccialetti* on your arm, rings of happiness. You hold on to a balustrade; this is the seventh floor. Behind you, the Basilica di San Nicola. Below, more cars than people in Toronto. The wall on your right is red. Perhaps an omen, but your grip is not firm. You wait for me to focus on your face. I am distracted by that wrinkle — sadness, disenchantment — tearing your cheek in two. It is siesta time, we are busy loving one another. You close your mouth, I still hear you speak. *Ti voglio bene*. I cannot hold you now. I am kilometers away from you, I have this image of you and an untouchable voice on the other end of the line. I see the photograph change but you remain always the same. You are my Molise in all her guises. You are Molise.

22 July 1984

Italia Mea Amore

They threw me out of my house,
they dragged me left and right,
from one room to another,
from one country to another.
They changed my name,
they cut the curls from my hair.
They laughed in my face
because I did not dress like them,
because I did not speak like them,
because I was neither white nor black.
They forced me to work
for a pay-cheque worth as much as spit.
They made me scrub washrooms
in factories, hospitals, cemeteries.
They raped my grandmother, my mother,
my sister, my daughter, my granddaughter.
They raped my father, my brother, my son.
They insured me, reassured me,
they fucked me good.
They put bread in my mouth
and told me I stole it.
They robbed me of my furniture,
money, job, wife and children.
They sent me to school
to learn the meaning of love, money and work,

they sent me to University
to learn how love, money and work were absurd.
They gave me a diploma
for losing my mother-tongue and history.
They taught me how to speak, swear,
study, steal, work, and think
in their language and history.
They took my meal away from me
and replaced it with bread and water.
They told me I was no one,
they told me I would find myself
in them by being like them.
They told me I was dead,
they told me you were dead,
they told me you were not mine.
They sold me drugs so I could forget
the colour of your eyes, the softness
of your skin, the warmth of your bosom.
They told me you were a whore,
a crook, a drunkard, an addict,
a hypocrite, a terrorist, a religious fanatic.
And when I called them the names
they had called you,
they spat in my face.
But it took just one look, one kiss,
one caress, one night beside you,
to rediscover myself
and understand what I am all about.
Now if they ask me my name,

I take the ink from your earth
and beside Antonio D'Alfonso
I sign *Amore*.

Montréal, 1 settembre 1984

ROMAMOR

Per Elena Fortuna

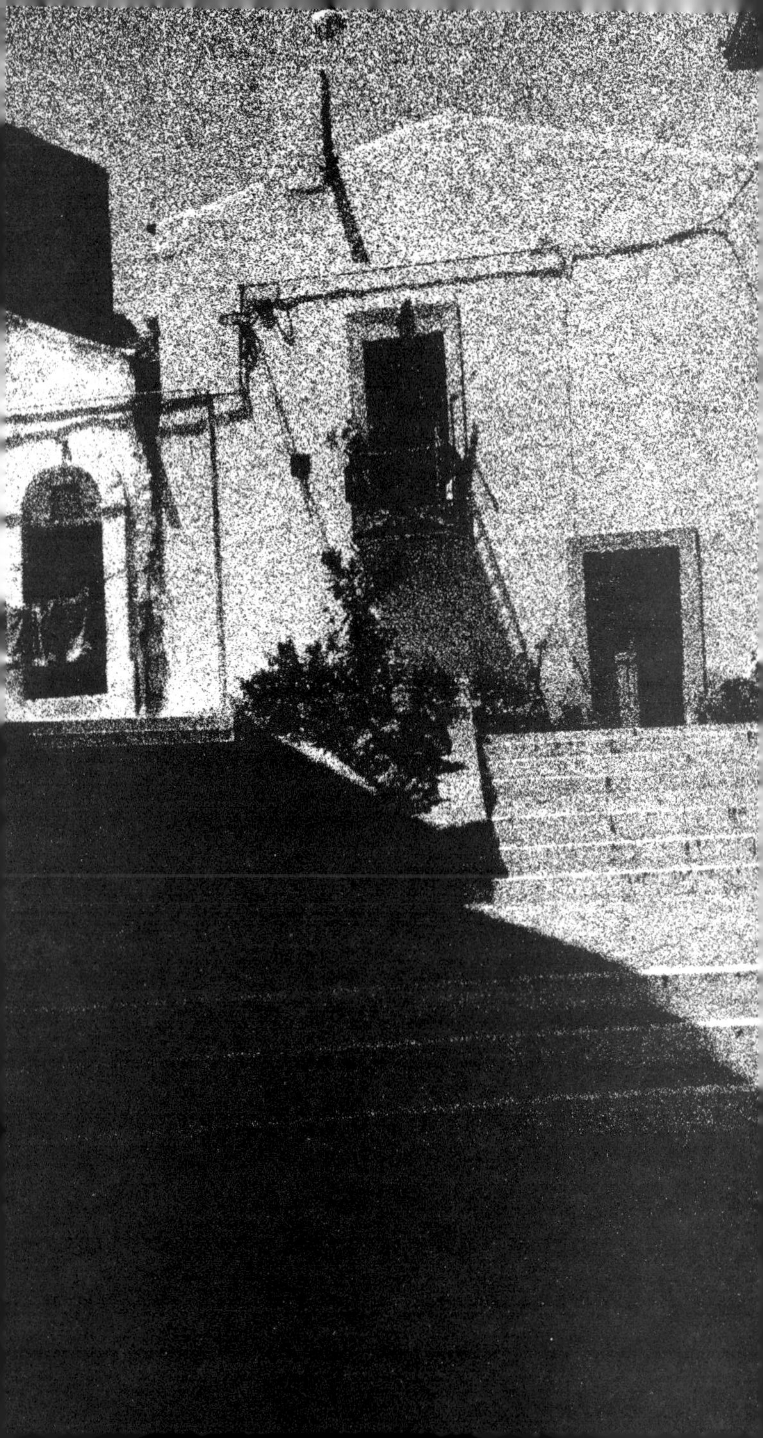

Comprends-tu que ce n'est pas toi qui la portes mais elle qui t'emporte là où tu n'aurais jamais cru qu'il soit possible de revenir — à des naissances continuelles.
Philippe Haeck
La Parole verte

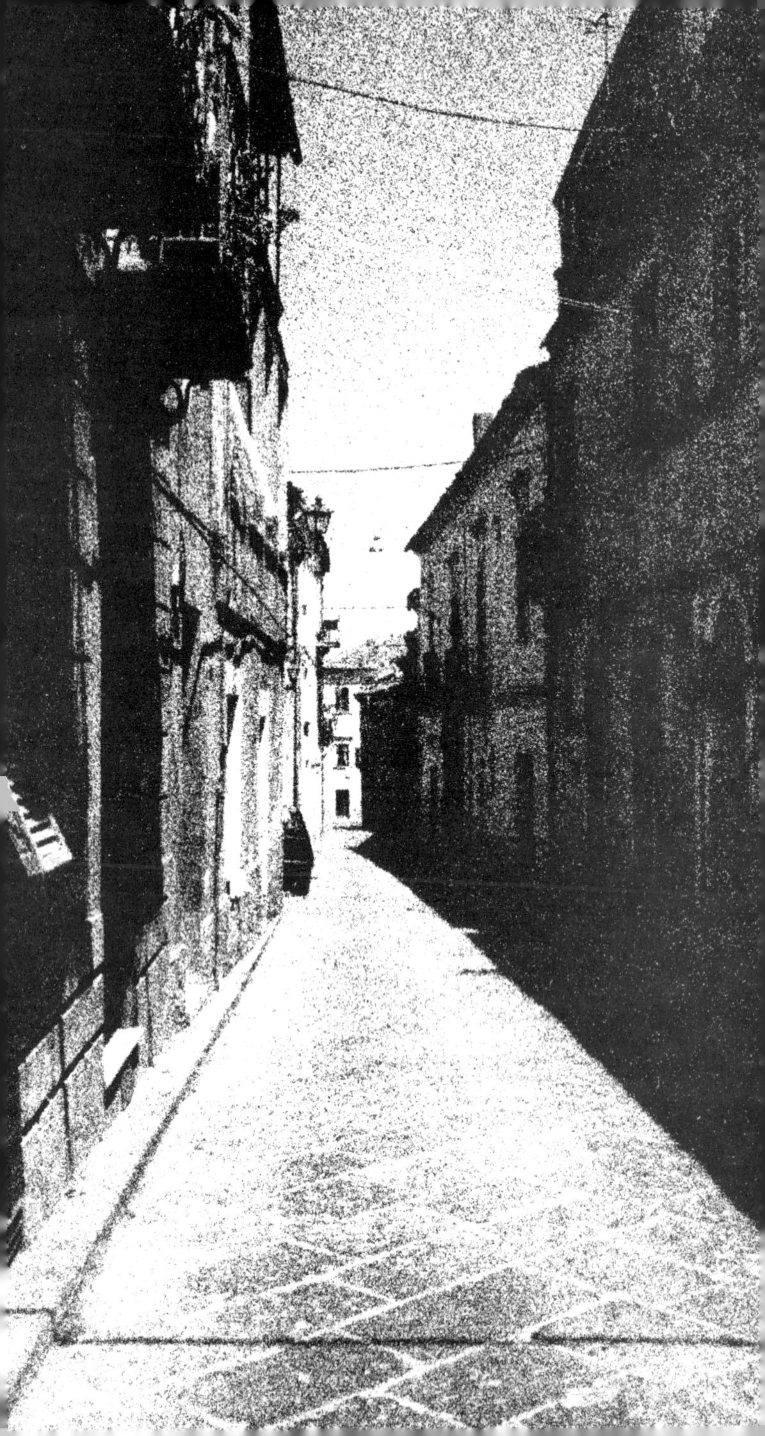

She

The sun shines
and tastes as bitter
as espresso coffee.

Her breasts, two
avocado pits rooting
in a glass of water.

Her lips open
like an umbrella.
She is a shelter.

Italia-Express

She says: *"Da quando sei in questo treno?"* He says: *"Una vita."* More than a means of locomotion; an experience in desire. Why does literature never cross the limits of our skin? The naming of lights, the emulation for the young, the train. An image more than the moving through time. An incomplete metaphor with no beginning, with no end. A conversation. Tuscany and Molise. An excuse for seduction. An apposition. Red, green, in between the blurry elements of white. To guess the red hair on her olive-coloured softness, her dark imponderables under my hand, the cosmography of sex. The train, balance goes berserk: our equilibrium.

13 October 1984

An Eroticism of Words

Fascination of language as landscape. The tactile experience of words. Imaginary: the physical relief of sentences. I listen but not to the meaning, only to the possible echoes of the language's genius. Why has language transformed my lifestyle? Listen to the muscles of mouths, lips, tongues, cheeks, throats moving. I love listening to you, *Amore mio*, when you move your body to my lips. Our love: a going towards the known, beyond the known. Concentration. Unconsciousness slipping out of ourselves. An eroticism of words. The horizon of our love.

Roma, 25 ottobre 1984

Our Continent

"The bed as an island, the kitchen table a continent. Invite your friends in, celebrate. Tonight's the night, my love: you are joking. What you expected would happen will happen. Sit beside me, tell me what you have been doing. Why have we not seen much of you these past days? Do not ask me to make love to you, I want to stay here in the kitchen and talk about whatever we think we will be doing on that island. If I go, promise to take me back here on this continent. I have been so confused, I do not know what is right or wrong anymore. I feel so natural when I am beside you. May I kiss your hand? Feel its security? I do not want this supper to end. I know these are lines one would not hear in the worst of films, yet I want to say them and pretend I am the only one to have ever said them. I feel better for doing so. Where shall we go tonight? Nowhere. Turn our bed into a continent, my love.''

Roma, 27 ottobre 1984

For Our Children

My red-headed heart, where were you when the Tiber overflooded its banks? What platform did you climb on to escape from drowning? Our hands, strong with will power, build better banks for our children to sit on and watch the green waters purify themselves. This is an era of science, my sister; we must know how to ask and answer questions of finance, architecture, emotions. We cannot say I do not know, I cannot care. What we have no one can cut down or burn. These are the buildings our children will inhabit.

Ostia, 29 ottobre 1984

Trees

In these houses all is removable. Nothing fixed. Except these moving people. Everywhere running around, their roots extending like elastic. A feast of mobility. This is why they invented emigration. Do you see those trees walking about, their branches carrying bags filled with fruits and vegetables? Lunchtime. This is the rush hour of empty stomachs — empty? These, forever hungry trees with in their arms little trees which will grow healthier and healthier. Saturday. One-thirty. The windows have been opened, the rooms are humid. The rain begins to fall. No sad faces, only trees turning greener.

Roma, Via Pio Foà, 27 ottobre 1984

Se son rose, fioriranno

Is this love of ours for nothing? It has no nationality and its critics — when they speak of us — have no cause to fight. We do not die, we do not think of suicide. Our love does not have esperanto for mother-tongue; nor is its goal to become androgynous. Its modus necessitates no sacrifice. If we leave, it is to return better. How will we keep this love alive? How will we keep our love growing from a distance? Writing letters? Long-distance phone calls? Come back to where we were an hour ago. We who were bastards have mapped the territory of our parents. We who were nothing have learned to become international lovers. *Se son rose, fioriranno*.

Ostia, 29 ottobre 1984

Bindings

Do not throw anything out the window. This is about being stable, in one place, here, land of the winged-horse, land of women on top of men, like the goat's head on the lion's back. Etruscan love. Who can throw a piece of his self out the window? Do not lean out, the oncoming reality will sever your head. Look at the distant castle on that mountain and think of history. This is no table shaken by returning ghosts. Think of love. Think of your people. You cannot live without your people, my love. I want to be the worm that bores holes in your soil. I want to be the red-roofed house on your green flag. I want to be the celestial ciment that binds your earth and sea together. I want to be whatever it is which binds earth and earth together. Your head on my lap, dreams like a breeze in your hair. I am slowly learning to bind my body to yours, and this is enough for now.

Arezzo, 18 November 1984

Will Passion Ever Forget Me?

Will passion ever forget me? In every fiber, on every table, on the bus, in a bar. Eating, drinking, kissing you. Passion. A passion play improvised. The scene filled with presence, absence. Actors waiting for the director to say Ok. Passion, *Amore mio,* in the cinema, tightening my fingers on the muscles of your thighs, your hand moving gently over my zipper. Passion you stretch your legs open putting your palms on my buttocks tightening yourself round me your tongue sticking out between your lips wet with our sweat calling my tongue sticking out between my lips wet with your sweetness passion the smooth cavity between your neck and breasts waiting for my fingers to come to rest there your shoulders my lips sucking the colours out of your freckles our passion the mirror image of this love RomaAmor this other side of desire I was looking for ROMAMO-ROMAMOROMAMOROMAMOROMA

Roma, 30 ottobre 1984

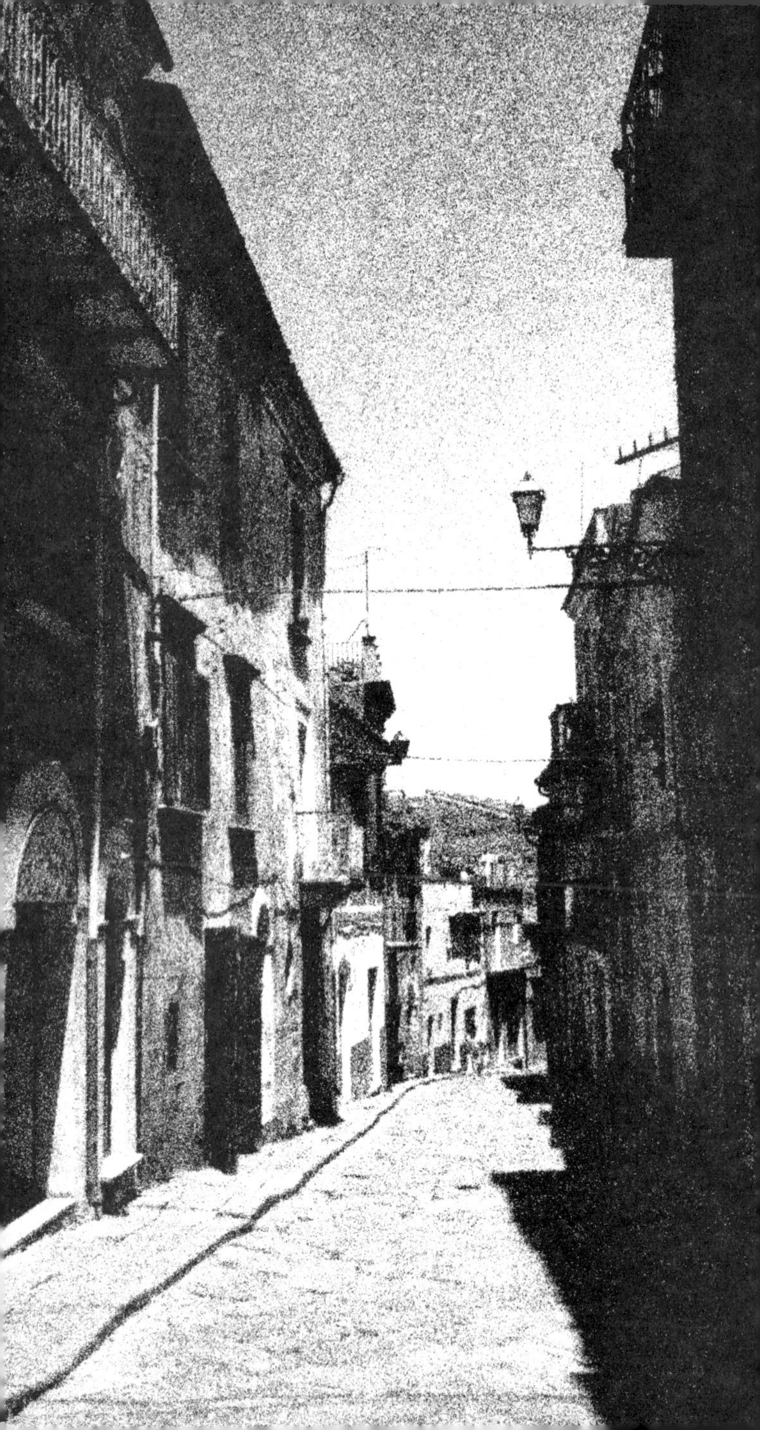

TO CRITICIZE ONESELF

À Patrick Straram

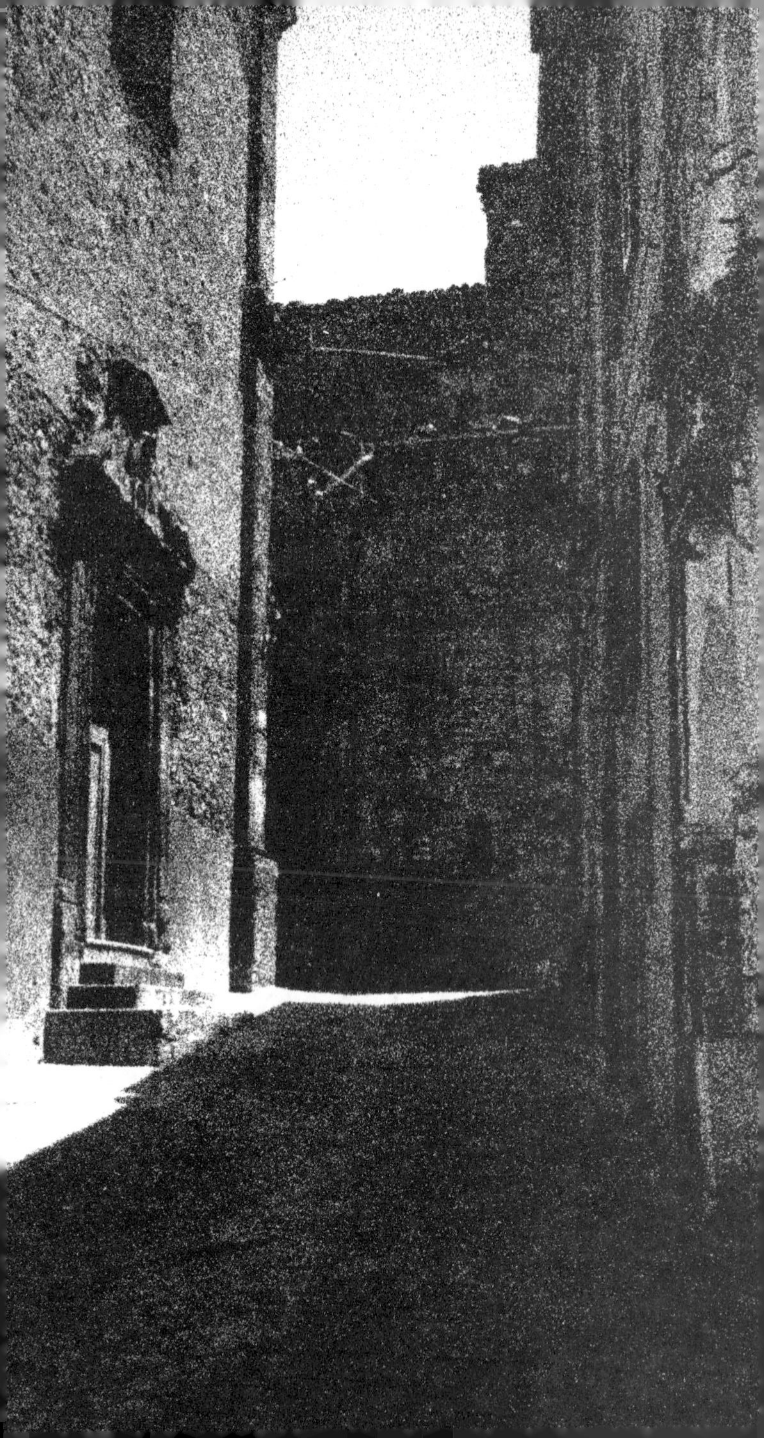

The Poverty of Money

How do you enter? Through the back or front door? If there are no doors, how do you walk in? You open a notebook expecting to find gold leaves, you laugh at the thought of comparing words to economy. Soon you realize gold has its own way of grabbing you by the collar, forcing you down to your knees. Karate and yoga will not get you out of its hold. It has pinned you and the count is over. Here is your self, there is your scream. Rats run through the cracks of your strength; no trap or image too violent to describe hope. Adjectives have no say in this play of the will where to know is ignorance. There are no rules, and you have no limits. The house is left abandoned; its doors slam shut and open — the wind as obstinate as you. If you are not invited, you break in like a terrorist.

17 March 1982

On Writing

1

Writing as memory. Writing also as a means of parring down reality to its essence. Writing which disclaims, whispers, breaks down. A way of speaking even when speaking entails narration. A narration necessitating expansivity, colouration, complexity.

2

Language a thing that contains itself. Not all language contains a priori memory. It may contain nothing at all. Language is overburdened with itself. It is energy propelling the user of language. Whether he likes it or not.

3

Language is never neutral. It expresses propagandistically what meaning a people has filled language with. To write is to remember the voices of your people, the voices of those who came before you. It is also a parameter reminding you of what can and cannot be done to your language.

4

To write is to remember. It is a memorandum of what you do to language physically.

5

No two people use language in the same manner. No two people use the same language in the same manner. These dissimilarities establish nations. The quality of being different is a matter of praise, not discrimination.

6

I can imitate the style of another writer. I can only emulate the stylistics expounded by writers of a certain era or century. In the end, however, I will find myself alone in front of the blankness of language. For language inevitably loses all its memory when it falls into the hands of a writer. Especially when the writer uses a language that is not his own, that is not the language of *his* people. *Difference.*

7

To record what I do to language: the impulse that pushes me to write. I write with the memory of one language in mind and express this memory in another language. It is the marriage of memories. I cannot write disregarding the Italian words I use to describe to myself the dazzling panoramas of man's command of nature seen from the heights of Guglionesi.

8

Even Italian is a learned language for me. Language of the North, it is not the language my thoughts got formed in nor the music I hear in my head at night when I cannot get to sleep. Already a transformation occurs: from Guglionesano, I must translate into Italian. When I write I translate. Sometimes no translation occurs. The words or phrases come directly into English or French. A linkage of differences.

9

A need for *bondage* and not assimilation of memories. A passion. A blind passion. An untempered impulse seeking science to carry it through pleasure. The sexuality of writing. The nonlinearity of the languages I bind together.

10

I do not break the natural flow of language purposely. It is the way language comes out of my body. Like breath. I breathe this way normally. When critics scorn my writing for being rigid, unnatural, I feel as if they are criticizing me for the way I breathe, for being the way I am.

11

Writing is intrinsically radical. What makes writers different from one another makes writing evolve, enriches the memory of a language and, ultimately, a people.

12

I am not American even though I find myself working here. Too often ashamed for being someone who stands out from the crowd, I have come to accept my difference. I am what I am and seek to express myself in the manner best atuned to the way my own flesh and bones express themselves. This, is my style. This, is the odour of my language.

13

I write to capture and describe the experience of not having language solidify itself inside me. The fluidity of language. Language as liquid.

14

If writing is memory, it is amnesia for readers. Why read a book if you keep the books of other writers in mind? Does a lover keep referring to other lovers when making love? The present moment as only truth. Reading: an exercise in forgetting.

15

To forget not only what comes before the book read, but also the line immediately preceding the line read. To question what one does naturally. To name one's style.

16

What interests me is not the naming of what I do as much as doing what has to be done. Writing is the memory, the *analysis* of what has to be done. Like video: writing captures and describes without theorizing on the thing captured and described. For writing to exist, it needs to be named afterwards. This is the work of the critic. No writing without the critic. The critic solidifies the fluidity of language.

17

To write, but also to analyse. To write, and to be read. Without the eyes of a reader, writing does not exist, cannot become memory.

28 June 1984

The Purity of Thinking

The express train. And no feeling of nostalgia. What produces this rear-view glance is the passion of landscapes. Room 6 as cozy as a washroom. Writing in a copybook placed on a chair opening to a toilet bowl. I stop writing and catch my reflection. To put on weight, to go beyond the comparing of the one I used to be to the one I have become. The snakes crawling in my stomach fall asleep. Not the destination, nor the departure. The hour between sleep and wakefulness. What brighter images than those wrapped by mist? What sharpness. A moment of clarity and uncertainty. No fixed thought, only the purity of thinking.

Toronto, 23 April 1983

For Louis Dudek

The deeper you go into memory, the deeper you go into language. And language belongs to origins. No, origins are not useless, but a source of personal identity. If "everyone you meet is a distant family relation", why have we built this Tower of Babel? What is useless is the vanity you might entertain on becoming *you*.

What makes you different from others, different from what others think you are, different from what yourself believe you are?

When I look back I do not look behind me. The past is not a house I have left behind. It is not behind me I will find my origins. Origins are all around me like skin, inside me like the pigment of my skin.

How do you acquire taste? The taste of becoming someone else? One morning, why do you wake up and feel obliged to move from one state of being to another, and then another still? Emigration, once it begins, never ends. Nomadicity.

"Don't expect a country to be built by emigrants. All an emigrant can do is help in the construction of railways, airplanes, roads, houses, hotels. You may convince an emigrant or two to invest, nothing more. The only country an emigrant fights for is the country of his heart and family."

This is not Utopia. This is not a base for a nuclear missile. An emigrant knows nothing of such fantasies. His country is the mother-tongue he wants his kids to learn, kids who can only scorn whatever it is that makes him what he is.

When I say *I*, I speak of a social environment inside and outside me. *I* is never alone. A family, a people, a dual nationality which in time of war suddenly becomes important. If I can search for what I am, it is because I never lost my self.

Sono quello che sono. I am what I am. A difference imposed on me by history. A way of living up to the standards imposed on myself by myself. Poetry, poetry, poetry... like the mechanical drills that bore holes in the soil of my history.

Guglionesi, 6 giugno 1984

New Economics

Irving Layton penetrated the tight muscles
of the genteel mind
and found freedom on the other side.
He felt racism strike down the heart
of his day, and cried.
I respect the man who cries
for he will bare no shackle
at his foot or in his brain.

Gaston Miron too cried; his sex smelled
like the earth of the North,
like the fresh air of the Artic.
He felt the rope tightening
round his throat, but his tongue
would not twist into the position
of hate. He has since built
a home he can be proud of.

If you are born without a home,
with a name ending in a vowel
that is poison in the mouths
of consonants, learn then from Layton
and Miron how not to round off
your accents or dye the colour of your skin.

Learn to speak the language of money
and know how to use it for singing.

11 December 1981

The Critic and the Poet

"I do not like this book. It suffers from an adolescent sensibility. There is too much extravagant lushness, which surrounds a core of nothing." The woman sits in front of him, distracted by the movement of his arms, the expression in his hands. "You are in love with words... you use words with Latin roots where a simpler Anglo-Saxon word would do." The woman thinks someone as unrefined as he is incapable of poetic intensity. People from his social stratum do not read or write. He takes a sip of his beer. "Much else in the volume is wordy ecstacy or agony, automatic writing clogged with portentous abstractions. Were it not for the stronger poems, one might question whether English was D'Alfonso's medium." A question mark. There is more poetry in one of his Italian grandmother's sayings than in a rich man's bank book. "How do you manage to reconcile poetry to your working-class background?" He does not know what she is talking about. "Your poems might have been something of a hit in Parisian suburbs, circa 1870, and some of them would no doubt have been smiled at by Baudelaire, possibly Voltaire. Interesting in content, lacking in depth. Images are manipulated to illustrate a concept, rather than being organic manifestations of insight." *Another silence grows into another song, another song grows into another silence.*

27 April 1983

Apatride

A musical composer, a painter, a sculptor, anything but this: a writer. When I come to my desk and pick up my pen, I never know what colour of ink to use, which dictionary to look into, what history book to copy. I wish I were someone born in a land which has seen his parents and grandparents working on that same piece of land, eating its fruit, building houses and bridges that always come back to the point of departure. But I was born to travel, to move without end from one house to another, crossing bridges to other shores, always a tourist, envying strangers tilling their land, building their houses and bridges. I am an eternal pilgram who will never say: *Me voici restitué à ma rive natale* (Saint-John Perse).

17 August 1985

To Criticize Oneself

Per Joe Pivato

He who aspires, he who inspires. Moving ahead. Concentration. Contentious. No idea more valid than another. Unanimity at times so perverse. Life cannot be deflowered, it can only blossom like a flower. Plunging itself into itself. Consuming its own existence. Finding essence in such mutations. In itself, with itself. Alone. Silent longing, because in all flourishes tenderness. Always the feeling of what it is that makes life worth living.

For the abyss then. Truth discovered in lies? Beauty in ugliness? What is ugliness? Suffering. Those that leave the person or thing they love. She leaves him because she loves him, so she says. A passing into presence. Naivety unfolding its genius. Pain cries its sun-rain pleasure. In laughter: realization of self. With others, through others, in others. "To go back to my country and make those I love happy." Land of good earth.

Criticize yourself because others cannot, will not. They too need to be criticized. How to accept that which we do not know? A word of faith? Those who are not frightened to criticize themselves know their way to freedom. Have they come from the shadows?

Poetry, history abstracting itself. Death of an excellent investment: what brings history and poetry together like lovers? What was said and written is re-inventing itself with the wind. Will the present ever last forever? Life offers itself to life and, as the wind blows through the almost extinct elm-trees, an interstice. It is dawn, as a flame.

27 March 1983

SIX

CA 10 GIUGNO

DORICO

OLONE

a Guglionesi

Europa

Et dans sa pensée deux voix égales, alternantes, qui jamais ne se rencontraient, se faisaient entendre à tour de rôle. Ces voix étaient contraires mais non pas ennemies.
Pierre Jean Jouve
Paulina 1880

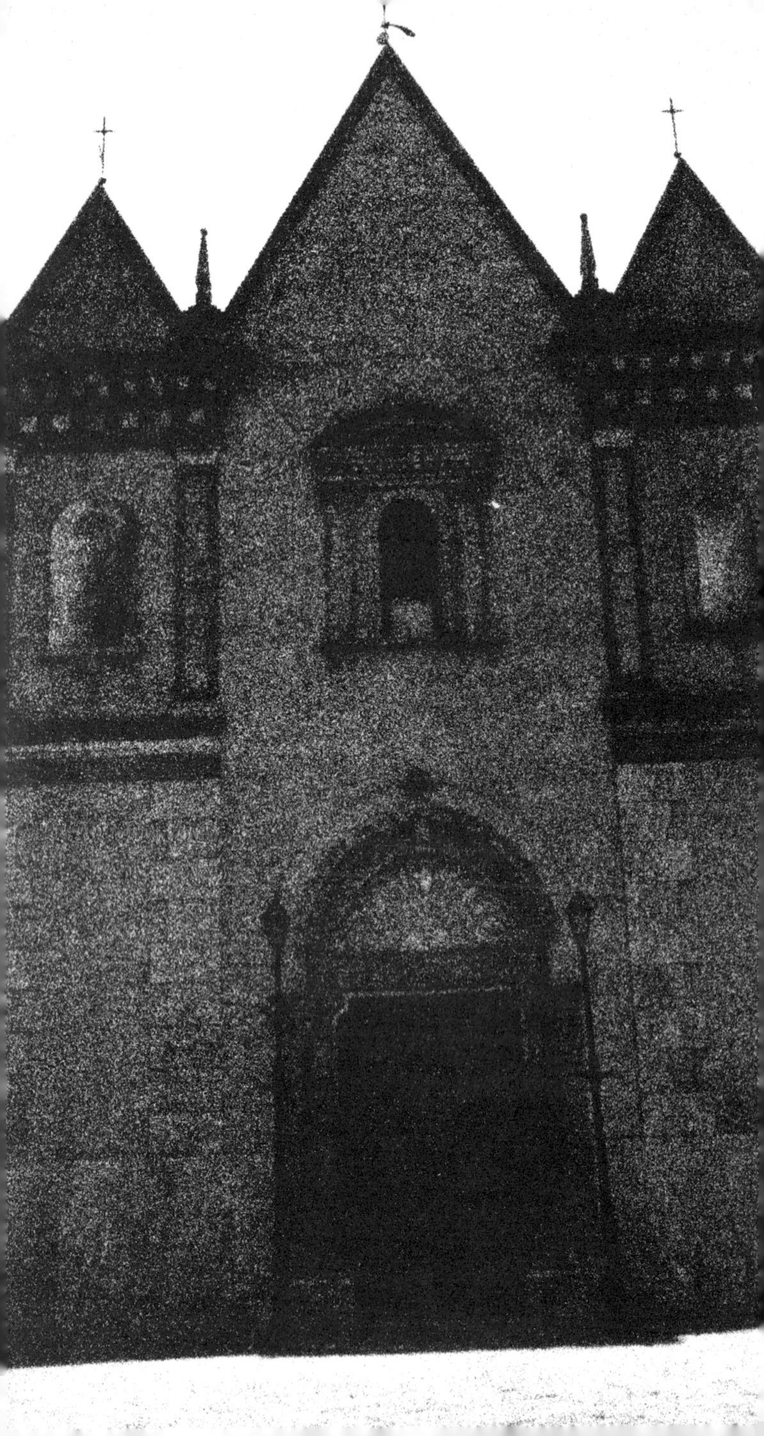

Roma-Montréal

Catholic city, God-forsaken cathedral, human strength of existential sacredness. Where buses stop, where tourists click their Nikons, where critics come to denounce this barbarian tombstone for those who fought to prevent their fellowmen from leaving their country. Not a stranger in this world of minorities. Look-out to the other shore, deeper in the deserts, calling. There is no country which does not open you the doors to another country. City on to city on to city. There is no innocent land, there is no natural land, only a desert to populate with language and history. O give me a ticket to the underside of the universe. Now that I have relearned the syntax of my breath. Now that the muscles of my mouth are relaxed, I want to study the languages of history. To see magic with my own eyes, to free the galaxy of its senseless celebrations of ignorance. My own grammar, my struggle with grammarless homes. Not nostalgia, just a revisiting of heaven before jumping down to hell. I have to dye myself with the ink of my imagination. The pleasure of finding being difficult. Roma-Montréal, to me the same, home of analysis and growth.

Roma, 22 aprile 1985

Roma

For Maria Di Michele

> *C'est un état de grâce*
> *varié par l'air moderne.*
> Claude Beausoleil

Roma. Rain. Roaming along Lungotevere. Past midnight. Under an umbrella too small for two. Going in circles in front of the Palazzo di Giustizia. The sky, one giant fountain. Trying to make sense of the past stolen from us. Born elsewhere, not from here. Always there, and the need to be here. Neither here nor there imagined as ideal. Our Utopia, the choice to be here and there. *Passim*. Roma. Rain. Roaming about Roman roads. Two Leos born on August 6. Speaking the feminine dialect of the masculine Fretani. History wrings us with its Baroque love. Perversity about being from nowhere. Antipatriotic. Blasphemous for this omnipresence of divinities. But we are not gods, for we have no place of comfort, no home to call our own, no hole to sneak into. We are balancing in midair like a direction sign loose at its hinges. We are dust blown from old furniture falling everywhere, nowhere. In which box to put our X? Roma. Rain. Roaming on Via della Conciliazione. Reconciling ourselves under Bernini's pillars, running on Vittorio Emmanuelle II's Ponte and Corso, stumbling into the Pink Bar where a gay Sardinian buys us a Scotch-on-ice for being from the Abruzzi. Two passports. Two persons in one. Lovers we never know who to kiss first. Who to speak to? What part to boast about? We suffer from insomnia. Who can we blame? "I wouldn't want to be in your shoes," repeats our friend, whose eyes jump from one body to another until they find the right bed to sleep in. "You'll end up looking like a portrait by Picasso." *Passim*. Roma. Rain. Roaming to the Piazza della Rotonda. Soaking wet with pleasure and schizophrenia, and what others call our *Ars poetica*. Will we ever quench our thirst? This grace with a modern air to it? At last

Vicolo del Divino Amore, drying ourselves to sleep in the folds of our measures.

10 giugno 1984

Barbara Engelmann in Arezzo

A*us der Zeit*. Angel of men in this city where were born Piero della Francesca, Francesco Petrarca, Giorgio Vasari. Arezzo: city of young men: Etruscan dreams like gold pins on dresses dropping to the marble pavement. A German poet living in an Italian poem. Walking beside me. In the cleansing rain. *Solo e pensoso? Ragionando con meco, et io co llui.* Via Italia intersected by Via Garibaldi. Thanking Garibaldi for his stubbornness.

I too celebrate unified Italy, I who fought against unity. I too sing one Italy, one people sharing one land. I too appear on this stage of communion and prayer. We enter the Duomo and *allora spavento ora tanta pace e interna luce* (Giorgio Vigolo). I am at peace with history. In Arezzo, southern hemisphere of the North! *Wer würde behaupten, Worte sind worte, Papier und Tinte*, whispers Barbara Engelmann, deciding to close her umbrella in the downpour. "This is not rain but Holy Water."

Arezzo, 16 novembre 1984

I Cannot Write as I Used To

Per Silvia

A chicken in madness, its head chopped off. The heart drowns in the wake of emotional traffic. A severed hand drops from the arm of a yellow raincoat. The tapping of purpose. That one sucks the syrup of forests is nothing. That one sucks pleasure out of harshness is nothing. Climax, exhaustion, fire are nothing, nothing, nothing. What hurts is the nod crushed like a fly by the hand, the palm, the fingers pulling inward, a cat on a leash, curling, a caterpillar from a stick, inward. Inward.

The things you say to yourself when you are alone, when you are in bed with your wife or lover, when you are getting a blowjob by the woman or man you have bought for fifty dollars.

The things you do not want to say to others, the things you do not want to say but do, the things you must not say but end up saying anyway, the things you should say but do not. The things, the things, the things.

I am fed up of this agony inside our gestures. I want to laugh at the tortures I inflict on myself, the pleasures you refuse to allow yourself to have. I want to stop pretending I am the protagonist of an Eisenstein film. *E salverei chi non ha voglia di far niente e non sa fare niente* (scrive Franco Battiato). I want to see myself dancing with the gypsies of the world, with all those who are no longer content with that which they possess. There is nothing to possess.

If your morals thicken, dilute them with saliva. If they are too watery, fix them with faith. Learn to reread what you thought you read well at first. I have images of *Metropolis* rushing on my brain's backdrop. I am falling and do not know what rhyming means. *Grace, drop from above* (writes George Herbert). What is all this commotion about? Keep your dirty laundry in your house.

I cannot write as I used to. It has become difficult for me to concentrate on the flow of images and how to make these images converge at a final point, the period that shall conclude this paragraph. Freeze frames. Forests on fire. Forest I walk in to lose myself. How does your husband touch you at night? Does he wait for you to come? I have lost my way tonight, my thoughts tangled like the hair of love, like the branches of the trees in love's forest. Show me the way to your heart of darkness, I know a flame burns for me there.

16 August 1984

Per Pier Giorgio Di Cicco

And the world he remembers forgives.
Pier Giorgio Di Cicco

I am balancing from one position to another. Outside I see only the blur of the passing landscape, lights shining in the horizon. The silence of wheels on steel tracks. *Fiumi e selve sappian di che tempre sia la mia vita, ch'è celata altrui.* Nothing in my head except the shadow of a weeping woman, the verses of Francesco Petrarca. "I want to burn my plane ticket in the Piazza Giordano Bruno." Zia Graziella tells me not to spit on Canada, not to say such things in public, though I may think them.

Wind inside a tunnel. Entering in the city whose guides say Romans are not brothers but distant relatives. The war between people who refuse unity.

There is no such thing as a unified country. I lift my glass to you, Pier Giorgio. Walk beside me along the crowded streets of Rome, let us drink the water that unites our energies and desires.

I think of you sitting at that café in Arezzo, drinking your fifth espresso of the day, telling me you need it because your blood is as black as coffee beans. I lift my glass to you and think of exile and emigration, and whatever it is that makes us tear our passports and run like shamans across the sky. I drink from your cup and hope for a loving community that will make blunt the prick scratching inside our brain.

Rain splashing against our foreheads. Nothing without a system, contradiction with its own logic. The geometry of rain. What is it that keeps our bones glued together, when the earth shakes in an epileptic fit? How many pages are needed to contain the immobile moment between confusion and taking a decision? *Se tu puoi, se tu vuoi, io pure lo posso e lo voglio.*

Train to Firenze, 15 maggio 1984

Ostia-Lido:
Per Pier Paolo Pasolini

Ostia-Lido: the sea, but also the limbo where you were killed, squashed on Via dell'Idroscala, on November 2, 1975. How could I forget this last city you visited, where you met death as a young man; where you met yourself, disfigured, chest crushed like the crushed carcass of a beetle. (Should I spell this B-E-A-T-L-E?)

Today *Panorama* dedicates ten full pages to you dead, in four colours, showing you in different poses: The Marxist, The Catholic, The Homosexual, The Anti-Abortionist. But about you The Man, alive, they chose to say nothing.

Pier Paolo Pasolini Killed by Pino Pelosi. So many P's make your death ominous. What power did your murderer discover inside the earth of your heart, inside the darkness of your guts? The sun, the sperm, the politics... the breaking of ciment covering sleeping buildings and flesh. The wind, the women dusting the furniture never used. The heart, the soap water spilt on brown marble pavements. Is this the Italy you fought to unite?

Crippled hands clutching cracked crystal champagne glasses applaud your sleepless night, your loveless bliss, your impatient stomach. What debt had you not paid, Pier Paolo? Saint Peter's or Saint Paul's? Or Pino Pelosi's? Or the organization working behind sex? The debt of poetry?

The debt of allowing your imagination to encompass the unencompassable.

21-22-23 ottobre 1984

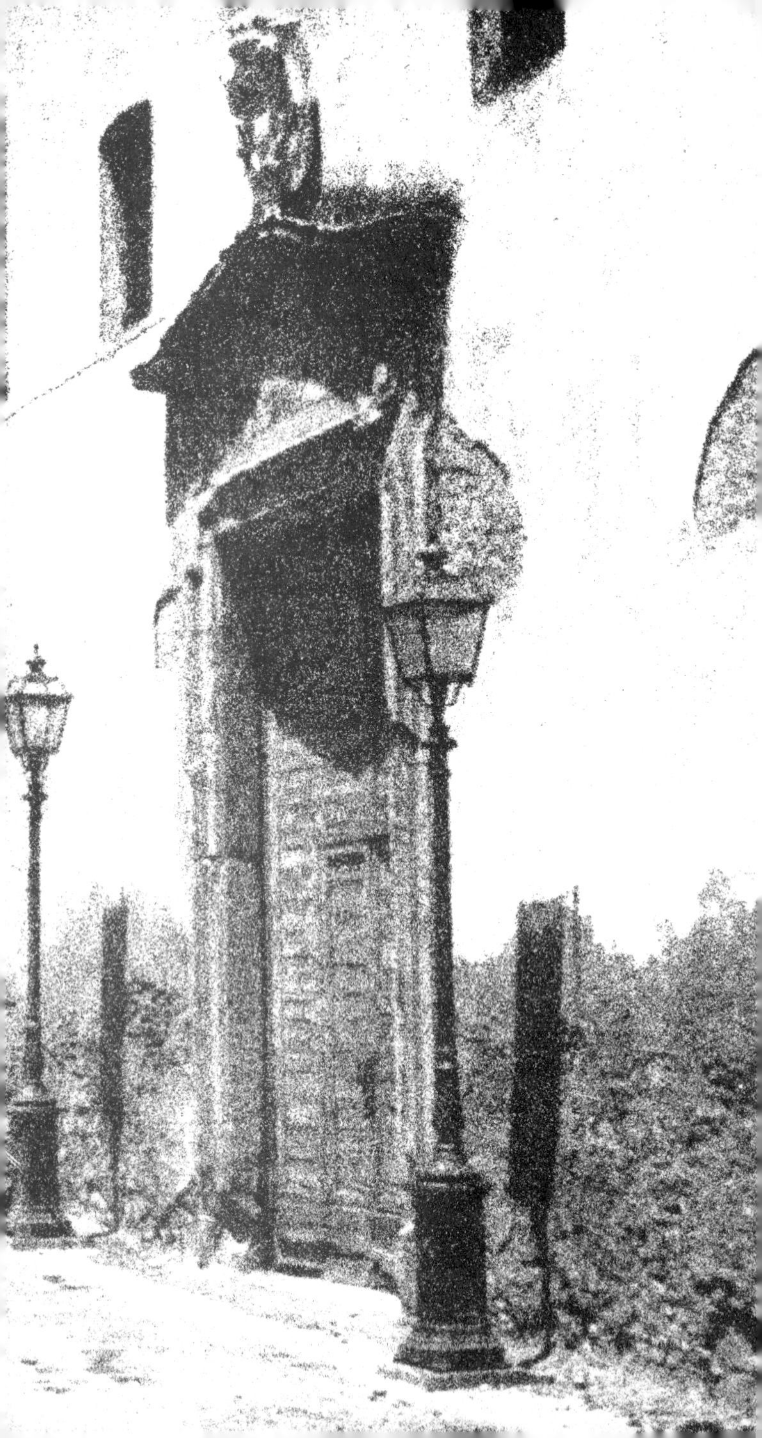

IL NUOVO
BAROCCO

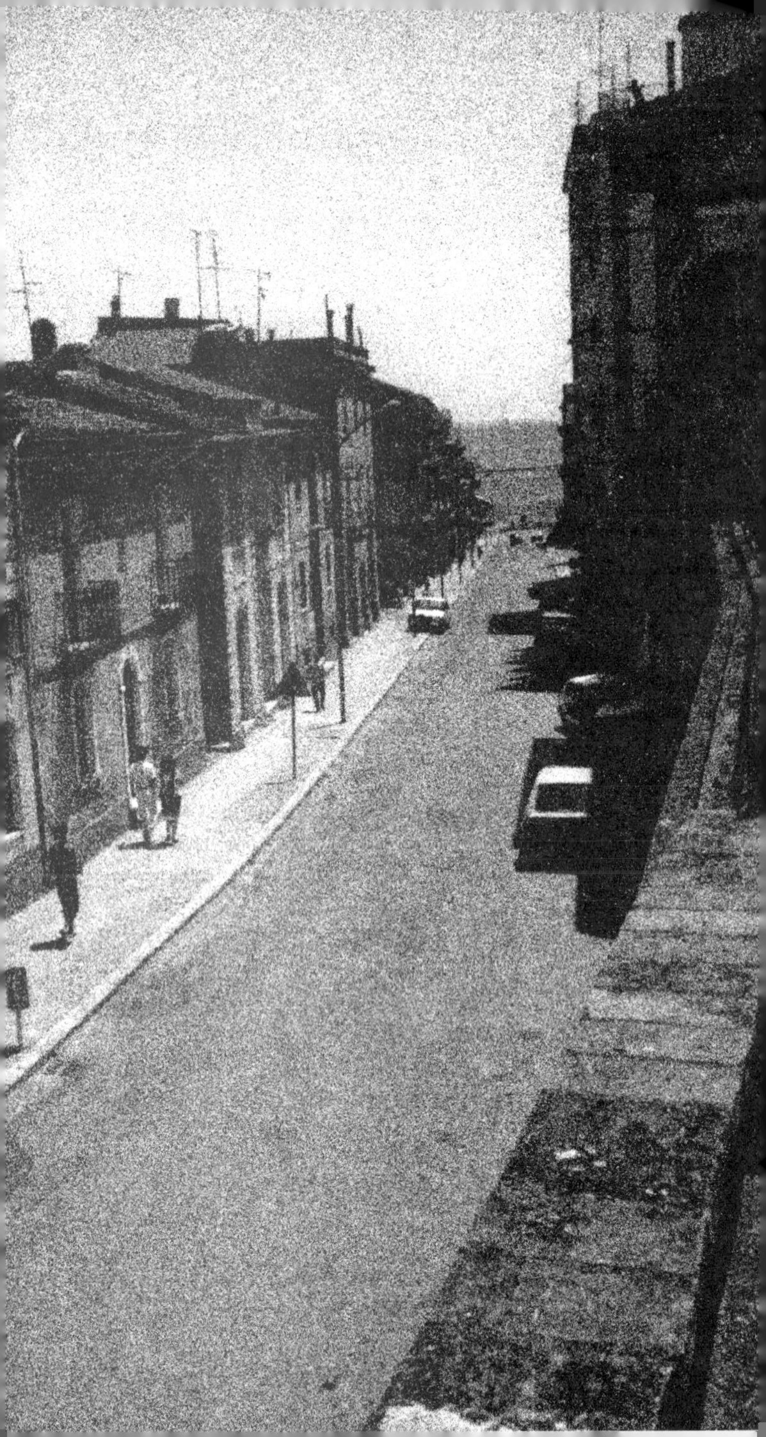

Il nuovo barocco

Sunday, 27 March 1984.

Saint Augustine. And so a text for Antonella D'Agostino with whom, in Rome, I learned to appreciate the Baroque.

Mina sings on the radio, her voice raucous, full of blues. I am sitting, thinking of how to cleanse this body of mine, free it of its blues. My cousin Tonino is sleeping, he refuses to get up. He tells me he feels he has carried a car-load of beans. He has done nothing physically since I have come to Guglionesi. His job: to entertain the family, offer it a little hope and show it new horizons, new directions. In the Baroque, life is as important as art.

Mina sings: *Rose su rose*. And I listen to my aunt scrub the marble pavement with vinegar. Marble: the Baroque; vinegar: bitter life? Bitter rice?

On my skin the freshness of a red-striped shirt. Today I decided not to wear an undershirt. I slip into cotton pants purchased in Florence, shoes purchased in Termoli — the sea, the sea — and a pair of white cotton socks. I feel like a real Italian here but I am embarrassed to feel this way. They have forced me to feel embarrassed about being Italian. In Canada we are not permitted to be what we are. I must get used to being what I am, inspite of the criticism such a decision will provoke.

Yesterday the Italian Azzurri beat Team Canada 2 to 0. Which team did the Italians in Canada cheer for? The American myth: Eldorado (or *Ladorada*).

I am reading Francesco Jovine. *Le terre del Sacramento*. Jovine is one hell of a high when read in Molise by a Molisano from abroad. Guardialfiera — Jovine's home town — is a few kilometers from Guglionesi. I can see Guardialfiera's landslide from my window.

Jovine understood his people well, their hopes, their fears. His work divided in scenes with dialogues is typically cinematographic. Very much like a mosaic. The Italian Baroque at its best.

Italian art is the essential expression of the Italian spirit. Vivaldi. Caravaggio. The Italian Opera of the Castrated Ones. Perhaps the unconscious expression of Italian art in Québec and Canada? How can we define Baroque art? (Re-read McLuhan and the history of the Baroque.)

B*arocco*: (from the Portuguese) an imperfectly shaped pearl. Seventeenth century artistic manifestations. Never the same, never expressed with the same intensity in every country. (Rembrandt and Vermeer belong to the seventeenth century as well.) It is an *ambiance*. A bizarre lifestyle, a bizarre way of thinking and creating. The Baroque: exuberance, ranting against the establishment, the harmonies of beauty and never-ending fashions. "Baroque art and poetry sought to unify disparate facets and experiences by directing attention to the moment of change" (McLuhan, *Through the Vanishing Point*).

To capture "the moment of change": the Baroque: the seventeenth century art of photography. I am thinking of Gianlorenzo Bernini, his *Model for Equestrian Statue of Louis XIV* (1670), his Vatican Collonade (1656). I am thinking of Francesco Borromini and his mosaic ceiling — that stares at God — in San Carlo alle Quattro Fontane. I am thinking. I am thinking again and again. To look at things differently.

Art, catch the fleeting moment. Caravaggio's "I musicisti". Photography's theatre. All that is useless in everyday life. How to find the essential in the absurd? Perhaps the Baroque is the *counterpoint* (Bach, and again Bach) of an essentialism I wrote of in 1977, describing the artistic outcome of returning to nature "to the power of two" — nature revisited — *retrouvée* — after having lived for so long in an urban and modern culture. The Baroque versus essentialism? No.

The Baroque is laughter coming from the artist who rediscovers nature, the innocent. The artist knows what an object is, what is absolutely necessary for an object to be an object, without which the object no longer is, becomes something else. Laughter, a possible solution in a world taking itself too seriously, drunk with theories which serve no other purpose than to force you deeper still into the absurdity of seriousness. The Baroque, that is the New Baroque does not contradict essentialism, it is another way of understanding essence, another way of catching essence which seems more and more fleeting.

5 September 1984.

Montréal. Saint Victor. Thinking about my uncle Vittorio with whom I slept, as a child, in our ''pig's sty''.

I am listening to Franco Battiato: *On a Solitary Beach*. I have decided to move on ahead. With my life. Nothing will stop me now. I will no longer bring myself to a halt. From now on, he who wishes can follow. The others can stay behind. Or ahead of me. (Moving ahead is not an experience that can be measured in inches.) Enough with my will to die. I must grab hold of myself. With the *passeggiata*. Once more that need to go for a walk. As if another world were opening before me. The world of words and thoughts. Going for a walk with a poet from Canada who speaks about nature ''to the power of two''. About essentialism. (Read the article I wrote on that poet to see how much I have changed.)

The term "baroque" has finally lost its negative connotations. "It has become a formula, historically individualized, to explain the lyrical expression of self, based on cleverness, wit, sententiousness which, in turn, is translated into a particularily refined and sumptuous form that privileges, at different levels, the rhetorical figure of the metaphor" (G.D. Bonino, *Il tresoro della poesia italiana*).

The Baroque: the period between 1580 and 1759. The New Baroque: the period between 1975 and —? So many artists to discover. To read. To re-read. Life cannot end here. Life begins anew. I find myself at a turning point in my life. Before another world. Deeper within myself. Deeper without myself. Deeper in my realities. The reality of one who laughs. I am thinking of Pier Giorgio Di Cicco. I am thinking of Marco Micone. I am thinking of Maria Melfi and Maria Di Michele. I am thinking of Marco Fraticelli. I am thinking of Carole Fioramore-David and Fulvio Caccia. I am thinking about how nice it would be to read them in Italian. Not because they should not write in English or in French, but because our realities can best be comprehended through Italian eyes.

I shall no longer write (in English). This notebook in which I move ahead. Alone. A step forward. A stop towards the ultimate horizon, the only path. To find myself. Ourselves. A step backwards.

The "moment of change": when one becomes another. The exact moment of transformation. The action fixed, the verb metamorphosing into a noun. The action and the verb possess a morality of their own, which rises from within; whereas the Baroque *freeze frame* — the artistic noun — knows nothing of morality. It exists per se and appears before our eyes naked, without pessimism or optimism, as if it were created by a mathematical force beyond our control.

Here all takes on meaning, even what seems useless. Therefore we cannot speak of superficial ornaments. All is fire without adjectives; the *benamed* being. A naming which does not need to explain its history for its past can be seen everywhere on the "face" of the fixed action and the captured emotion.

If the Baroque is lyricism, it is one free of the romanticism of action, free of the automatism of modernity whereby action presents itself as an excuse or the ultimate outcome of the magical moment. In the New Baroque action counts no more. The beginning and the end emerge from the same moment, incorporated in it, its narration intrinsically fused to its mutation. We may compare it to British seventeenth century metaphysics — as in George Herbert and John Donne — for in these works we find a mad desire to fix a process which includes its beginning and end, and is proposed as a manifestation of being, half dead, half alive, without a before, without an after: a being manifests itself here naked, with its entire history.

If modernity expresses the dramatization of the moment, that is the quest to eternalize the "dramatic moment" of the artistic act, the New Baroque refuses such drama and attempts to communicate essence dramatically in a most vigourous performance. After modernity — urban nature or urbanism as nature — begins the New Baroque which does not distinguish between nature and urbanism between action and essence. The New Baroque is the fiction of fiction, eyes looking at eyes looking, a creative paranoia characterized by distrust in matter and art (reality and the narration of this reality in linguistic and non-linguistic terms).

The New Baroque regards modernity and tradition as belonging to a single reality; it therefore refuses to envisage metalinguistics as the only solution to contemporary art.

The New Baroque, the art of the white clown. (San Francesco d'Assisi. All these saints as metaphors of our occidental world. Language on the language of reality.)

Laughter. (Re-read the history of comedy. Read Henri Bergson's *Le rire*. Go back to see Toto's films and those by the young Fellini. See again and again *Francesco, giullare di Dio* by Roberto Rossellini, co-scripted by Federico Fellini. And how to forget Charlie Chaplin, Jacques Tati?)

Laughter.

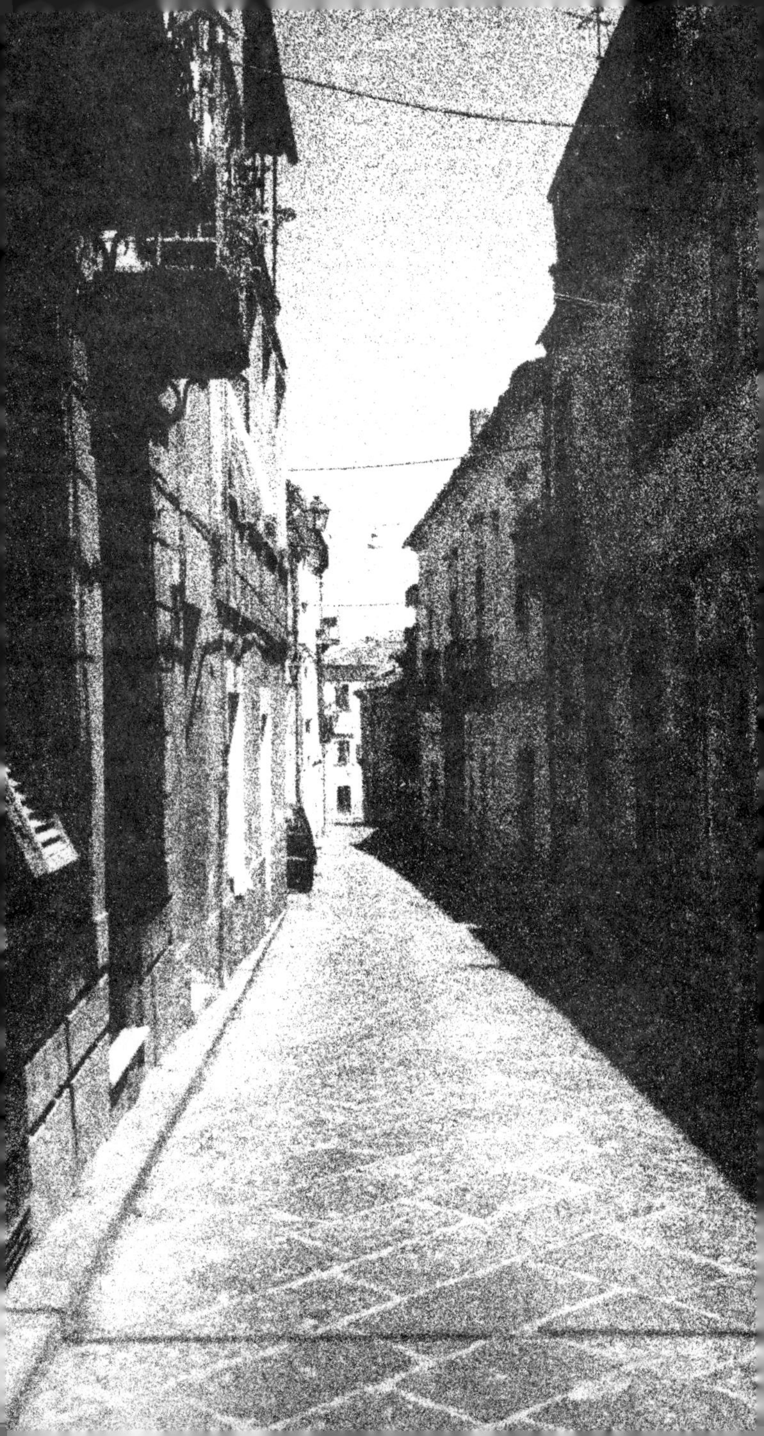

By the Same Author

La chanson du Shaman à Sedna (1973)
Queror (1979)
Black Tongue (1983)

Quêtes:
Textes d'auteurs italo-québécois (1983)
(avec Fulvio Caccia)

Voix Off:
Dix poètes anglophones du Québec (1985)

The Clarity of Voices
Selected Poems 1974-1981
(Translation of Philippe Haeck's prose poems, 1985)

L'autre rivage (1987)

L'Amour panique (1988)

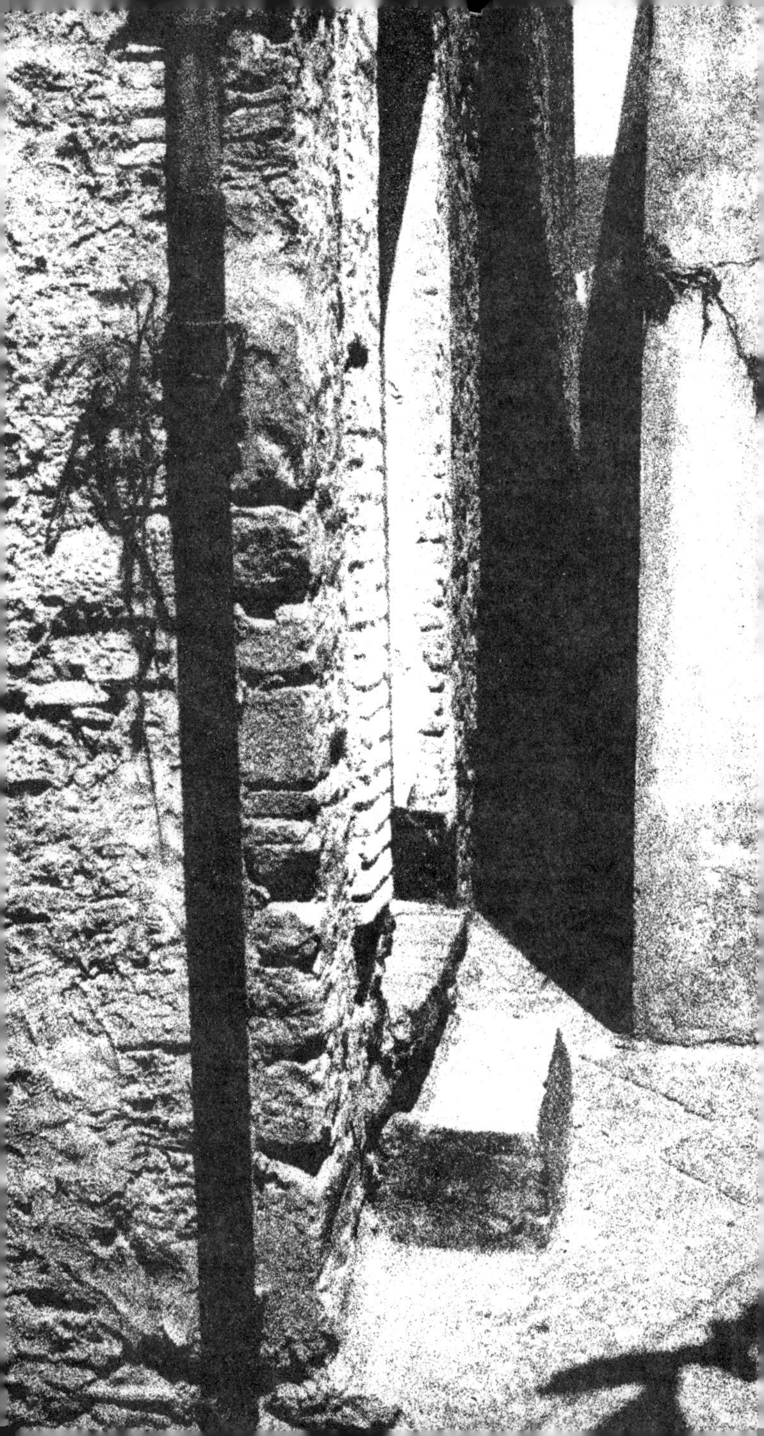

Printed by
the workers of
Ateliers Graphiques Marc Veilleux Inc.
Cap-Saint-Ignace, Qué.